# A–Z

of

# RIBBON EMBROIDERY

SEARCH PRESS

First published in Great Britain 2016

Search Press Limited
Wellwood, North Farm Road,
Tunbridge Wells, Kent TN2 3DR

First published in Australia by Country
Bumpkin Publications
© Country Bumpkin Publications

ISBN: 978-1-78221-173-0

**Suppliers**
If you have difficulty in obtaining any of the
materials and equipment mentioned in this
book, then please visit the Search Press
website for details of suppliers:
www.searchpress.com

Printed in China

# Contents

# General information

## Ribbons

Where once ribbons were limited, expensive and difficult to obtain, today, ribbons come in a wide variety of types, colours, widths and appearances.

Ribbons are available in widths ranging from 2mm (⅛") through to 50cm (2"). When working on large-scale designs, it is best to use the wider ribbons. Combinations of different widths and textures in ribbons can be most effective, so choose the ribbons for the particular effect you wish to achieve and buy the best quality you can afford.

As some damage can occur when pulling the ribbons through the fabric, they need to be very strong, yet lightweight. It is worth considering the following characteristics of ribbon types before you begin embroidering.

### Silk ribbon

Silk ribbon is the most popular choice. This soft, pliable ribbon can produce fine, delicate work. It has a soft grain and scrunches readily. Bias cut silk ribbon has the added advantage of being easily moulded as it has the same draping properties as bias cut fabric. Interesting effects can be created by fraying its edges.

### Synthetic ribbon

This type of ribbon is coarser than silk ribbon and gives a heavier look. It has much more bounce and will not compact to the same degree as silk ribbon. Polyester and rayon-acetate ribbons are often manufactured with tiny wires woven into the selvedges, enabling the ribbon to be shaped and formed in a distinct way.

### Cotton ribbon

Grosgrain ribbon, often used in millinery, is rarely used in ribbon work.

### Satin ribbons

Satin ribbons can be made from either silk or synthetic fibres. It is the special weave of these ribbons that gives them their distinctive characteristics.

Double sided satin ribbons are relatively inexpensive and particularly suited to techniques where the ribbon is folded so that both sides of the ribbon show. Double faced ribbons have a different colour on each side. Ribbons that have a satin finish on one side and a rough finish on the other can also add texture and charm when folded.

### Sheer ribbons

Fancy sheer ribbons, such as spark organdy or georgette, are useful for their transparency and add an extra dimension to an embroidered piece.

### Textured ribbons

Textured ribbons, such as plush velvet, can add lustre to the design through their richness.

### Hand dyed ribbon

There are several types of ribbons available that are hand dyed and these ribbons display wonderful effects. For added interest, try working with variegated ribbon, where the ribbon will change from one colour to another. A more subtle choice is ombre or gradated ribbon, where the ribbon blends from one shade to a lighter shade within one colour range.

## Fabrics

Almost any type of fabric is suitable for ribbon embroidery and should be chosen for the effect you wish to achieve. However, when planning your piece, some consideration needs to be given to the other forms of embroidery you will be using in combination with the ribbon work.

Select fabric that is firm enough to support the stitching, but with a weave loose enough to allow the ribbon to pass through the fabric without becoming damaged. Fabrics with abrasive fibres should be avoided.

## Needles

Needles are numbered with the highest number being the smallest needle in the size range.

The needle should make a hole in the fabric that is large enough for the ribbon to pass through easily. The hole should allow the ribbon to spread out sufficiently once the stitch has been formed. Using too small a needle will wear and fray the edges of the ribbon.

Recommended needles to use have been included in the instructions for each project.

### Chenille needles

Available in sizes no. 13–24, these needles have a large eye, thick shaft and a sharp point. They are suitable for most stitches, but especially ribbon stitch, where the needle must pierce the ribbon to complete the stitch. Use the smaller number needles for the wider ribbons and the large number needles for the narrower ribbons.

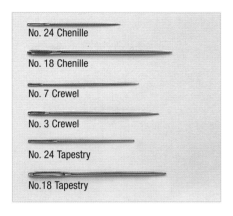

No. 24 Chenille

No. 18 Chenille

No. 7 Crewel

No. 3 Crewel

No. 24 Tapestry

No.18 Tapestry

### Tapestry needles

Tapestry needles have a broad eye, and a blunt point. They are very useful for stitches that require the needle to pass between a ribbon stitch and the base fabric. The blunt end avoids snagging the ribbon or fabric with the needle.

### Crewel needles

Having a slender eye, thin shaft and sharp point, these needles are used for stitching with machine sewing thread or stranded threads. Larger crewel needles can be used with narrow ribbons.

## Tools

### Hoops and frames

Whether to use a hoop or not is very much a personal choice, however the best results are achieved when the background fabric is held under tension. Use small hoops that are easier to handle and, when positioned correctly, avoid flattening the finished sections of the embroidery.

If choosing to use a scroll frame or stretcher bars, ensure it is large enough to cover the entire area of the design. Free-standing frames are also useful as both hands are free to manipulate the ribbons. No matter whether you choose a hoop or a frame, a good quality one will hold the fabric firmer than a cheap one.

# THREADING THE NEEDLE

This easy method ensures the ribbon is secured firmly to the eye of the needle, ready to begin stitching.

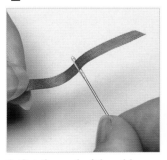

**1** Cut the end of the ribbon diagonally. Thread the ribbon through the needle eye. Slide needle along ribbon for approx 5cm (2").

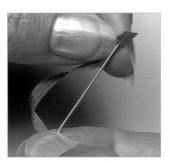

**2** Place the point of the needle approx 5mm (³⁄₁₆") from the cut end of the ribbon.

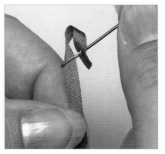

**3** Push the needle through the ribbon. Holding the tail in one hand, pull the needle with the other until a knot forms at the needle eye.

**4** The ribbon is now secured and you are ready to begin stitching.

### Stiletto or awl

These are helpful to puncture holes in tightly woven fabrics or where wide ribbons are used. This process of making a hole first reduces the wear on the ribbon.

### Cylinders

Items such as drinking straws, chopsticks and shaslik sticks are useful items to have in your ribbon embroidery tool kit. When placed under ribbon while stitching loops, they help add height and ensure the stitches are even.

### Ribbon weaver

A ribbon weaver can be used for much the same purpose as a tapestry needle. It is flatter than a needle and will not disturb previously laid ribbons when weaving under them.

### Rubber grip

Use a piece of fine rubber, or even a small square from a balloon, to grip the needle when pulling ribbon through tough sections.

### Transferring designs

There are many ways to transfer a design depending on the type of fabric you are using. For ribbon embroidery, a very simple outline of the design plus placement marks or dots for the largest elements within the design are all that is needed. Too many marks tend to become confusing and can be difficult to cover. As an example, use a single dot or circle to mark the position for the centre of a flower, rather than drawing the complete flower.

### Methods of transfer

#### Direct tracing

This method is suitable for fabrics that are light in colour and relatively sheer. Trace the design onto tracing paper. Place the design under the fabric on a flat surface. Tape both the fabric and the tracing to the surface and mark the design onto the fabric with a suitable medium. Taping to a window or light box will make it easier to see the design lines.

#### Tacking

Although time consuming, this method gives the most satisfactory result as it leaves no permanent mark. Trace the design onto tracing paper. Pin the tracing, design uppermost, onto the right side of the fabric. With contrasting thread, tack along the design lines with small running stitches. Score the tacked lines with the tip of the needle and tear away the paper. Remove the tacking as you work.

### Fabric markers

#### Fabric marking pens

These markers are non-permanent and are suitable for fabric with a smooth surface. They are not suitable for framed pieces as the ink may reappear. It is important to read the manufacturers' instructions carefully.

#### Lead pencils

Use a sharp, medium to soft lead pencil for light coloured fabrics. For dark fabrics, use a soft white pencil. Draw the lines lightly onto the fabric.

#### Chalk based fabric pencils

These types of markers are excellent for dark fabrics and will brush or wash off. Do not use on fabrics such as silk, where watermarks may be a problem. The chalk tends to brush off quickly as you work.

## Special hints

Before use, test ribbons for colourfastness and wash if necessary. Using short lengths of ribbon helps to prevent damage caused by continually passing the ribbon through the fabric. Cut ribbons no longer than 30cm (12").

If using a hoop, do not leave the work in the hoop when not embroidering.

When the embroidery is complete you may need to give the piece a final press. Place the piece face down on a well padded surface. Lightly press around the design, taking care not to press the ribbon. If the piece still needs pressing, and depending on the ribbons used, stretch the work onto a quilter's board or similar and pin. Lightly mist with water and allow to dry.

# Stitches and techniques

A wide variety of ribbons can be used for each of the stitches and techniques included in this section.

Using ribbons of different widths and types will often alter the look of the finished stitch, so it is worth experimenting on a sampler before committing a new stitch to your design.

In almost every instance, it is important to ensure your stitches are longer than the width of the ribbon you are using.

Stitches shorter than the width of the ribbon will appear narrower as the ribbon is not able to spread to its full width.

# BULLION KNOT – DETACHED CHAIN COMBINATION

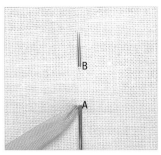

**1** Bring the ribbon to the front at the position for the base of the stitch (A).

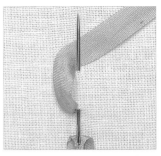

**2** Take the needle to the back of the fabric just to the right of A and re-emerge at B. The ribbon lies to the left of the needle.

**3** Take the ribbon from left to right behind the tip of the needle.

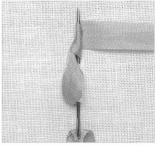

**4** Keeping the ribbon flat and untwisted, wrap it around the tip of the needle in a clockwise direction.

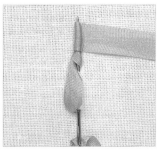

**5** Pull gently so the wrap lies snugly against the needle but is not tight.

**6** Repeat steps 4 and 5 for the required number of wraps. Ensure the ribbon around the needle is smooth.

**7** Hold the wraps in place (thumb not shown). Pull the needle through, carefully easing the wraps over the eye of the needle.

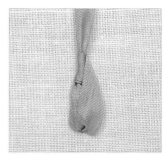

**8** Pull until the ribbon forms a firm bullion knot at the end of the detached chain.

**9** Take the needle to the back of the fabric at the tip of the bullion knot.

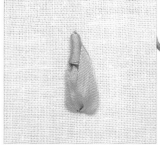

**10** Pull the ribbon through and end off on the back of the fabric. **Completed bullion knot – detached chain combination.**

8

# COLONIAL KNOT

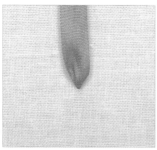

**1** Secure the ribbon on the back of the fabric. Bring it to the front at the desired position for the knot.

**2** Hold the ribbon loosely. With the right hand, take the needle tip over the ribbon.

**3** Hook the needle under the ribbon where it emerges from the fabric.

**4** With your left hand, take the ribbon over the tip of the needle. Shorten the loop around the needle.

**5** Take the ribbon under the tip of the needle. The ribbon now forms a figure eight around the needle.

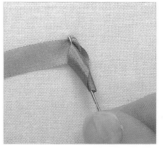

**6** Take the tip of the needle to the back, approximately one or two fabric threads away from where it emerged.

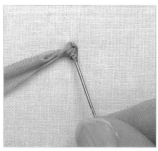

**7** Pull the wraps firmly against the fabric and begin to take the needle to the back.

**8** Keeping the ribbon taut, continue to push the needle through the knot to the back of the fabric.

**9** Holding the knot and loop on the fabric with your thumb, continue to pull the ribbon through (thumb not shown).

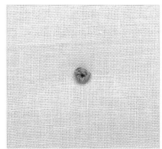

**10 Completed colonial knot.**

# CONCERTINA ROSE

This rose is particularly effective when worked in double-sided satin ribbon. It has lots of body and as the ribbon is folded back and forth, both sides show. Prepare a needle threaded with matching sewing thread before you start.

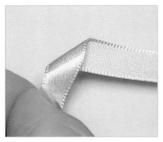

1 Fold the ribbon at right angles at the centre. Hold the fold in place.

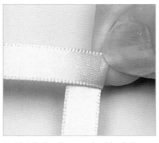

2 Fold the lower half of the ribbon over, keeping it at right angles to the upper half. The fold is at the edge of the ribbon. Hold in place.

3 Again, fold the lower half over the upper half, ensuring the fold sits at the edge of the ribbon. Hold in place.

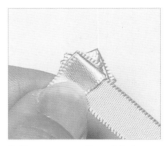

4 Repeat steps 2 and 3 the desired number of times (we repeated the steps seven times, ie folded the ribbon over fourteen times).

5 Hold the two ends of ribbon firmly in one hand and release the folds.

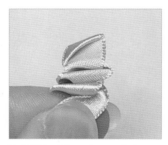

6 Still holding the ends in one hand, begin to pull one end with the other hand.

7 Continue pulling the same end until the rose forms and the folds sit close to your fingers.

8 Hold the two ends together. Using the sewing thread, take the needle through both pieces of ribbon close to base of the rose.

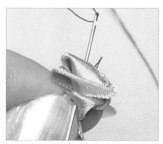

9 Pull the thread through. Take the needle from the base up through the centre of the rose.

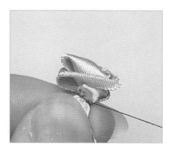

10 Pull through. Take a tiny stitch and take the thread back through the centre to the base. Wrap thread around base approx three times.

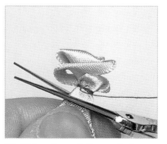

11 Take thread through base and end off. Trim excess ribbon, leaving a small stump.

12 Press stump flat with thumb. Attach rose to fabric by taking tiny stitches through the base and stump. **Completed concertina rose.**

# COUCHING

A wide variety of stitches can be used for couching ribbon. Your choice will depend on whether you want the couching to be decorative or purely functional.

1 **Laying the ribbon.** Bring the ribbon to the front of the fabric.

2 Smooth and spread the first section of ribbon by moving your needle behind it while applying a slight upward pressure.

3 Lay the ribbon on the fabric in the desired position. With a pin, pick up a tiny amount of fabric on one side of the ribbon.

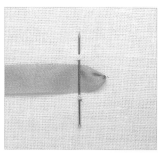

4 Take the pin over the ribbon and pick up a tiny amount of fabric on the opposite side.

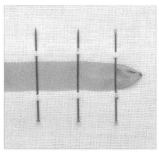

5 Continue pinning in the same manner at frequent intervals or where the ribbon changes direction.

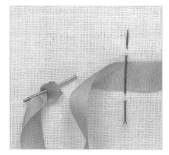

6 When near the end, take the ribbon to the back of the fabric.

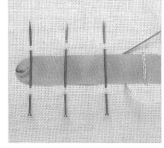

7 Pin the last section in the same manner. Couch the ribbon with the desired stitch, removing the pins as you come to them.

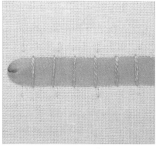

8 **Completed couching.**

9 Ribbon couched with French knots.

10 Ribbon couched with herringbone stitch.

11 Ribbon couched with stab stitch.

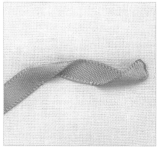

12 Ribbon couched at the folds with stab stitch.

# DETACHED CHAIN

Also known as lazy daisy stitch and daisy stitch, detached chain is a looped stitch. Different effects can be achieved by the way the ribbon is positioned around the needle.

## Method 1  Method 2

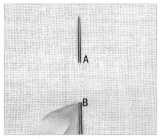

**1** Bring the ribbon to the front at A. Take the needle to the back of the fabric as close as possible to A and re-emerge at B.

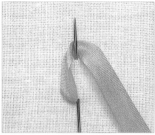

**2** Loop the ribbon behind the tip of the needle.

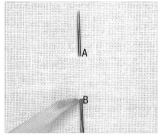

**1** Bring ribbon to front at A. Take the needle to the back of the fabric as close as possible to A and re-emerge at B.

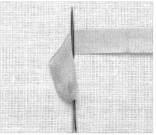

**2** Take the ribbon behind the tip of the needle, folding it away from you and diagonally as shown.

**3** Begin to pull the needle and ribbon through.

**4** Continue pulling until the loop is the desired shape. The tighter you pull, the narrower the ribbon will appear.

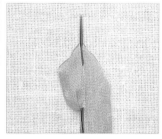

**3** Fold the ribbon towards you as shown.

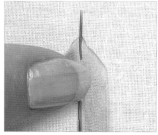

**4** Position your thumb over the ribbon to hold the folds in place.

**5** Take the needle to the back, just beyond the loop.

**6** Pull the ribbon through. **Completed detached chain.**

**5** Gently pull the ribbon through.

**6** Take the ribbon to the back of the fabric, just beyond the loop. **Completed detached chain.**

# DETACHED CHAIN – TWISTED

Twisted detached chain is a variation of detached chain and can be worked with either ribbon or thread.

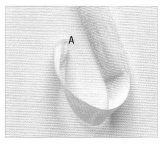 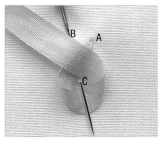 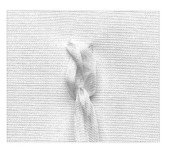 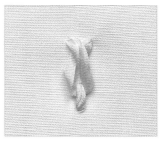

1 Bring the ribbon to the front at A. Make an anti-clockwise loop. Hold the loop on the fabric with your thumb (thumb not shown).

2 Take the needle to the back at B, just to the left of A. Re-emerge through the loop at C.

3 Ensure the ribbon is smooth and untwisted. Carefully pull the needle through until the loop gently tightens around the ribbon.

4 Take the needle to the back of the fabric just over the loop. Pull the ribbon through. **Completed twisted detached chain.**

# FLY STITCH

By varying the tension and smoothness of the ribbon, the length of the anchoring stitch and the distance between the 'arms', many different looks can be achieved with this one stitch.

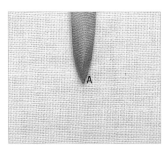 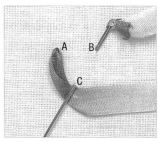

1 Bring the ribbon to the front at A. This will be the left hand side of the stitch.

2 Take the needle to the back at B and re-emerge at C. Loop the ribbon under the tip of the needle.

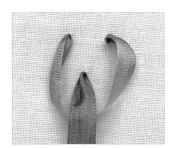 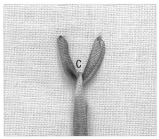 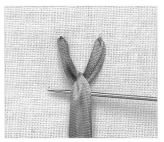 

3 Gently pull the ribbon through. If desired, ensure the ribbon is untwisted.

4 Pull until the looped ribbon rests against C.

5 Smooth and spread the ribbon moving the needle behind it with a slight upward pressure.

6 Take the needle to the back of the fabric and pull the ribbon through to anchor the stitch. **Completed fly stitch.**

# FOLDED RIBBON ROSE

1 Prepare a needle threaded with matching machine sewing thread. Put a small knot in the end.

2 **Centre.** Hold the ribbon horizontally. Fold over the right hand end diagonally so you have a tail of ribbon approx 1.5cm (⅝") long.

3 Holding the ribbon with your left hand and the folded tail with your right, roll the fold firmly in a clockwise direction for one turn.

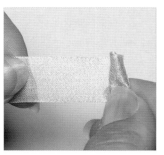

4 Roll twice more to form the centre of the rose.

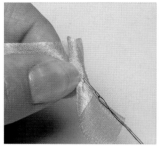

5 Still holding firmly and using the thread, take the needle through all layers of ribbon at the lower edge.

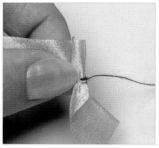

6 Pull the thread through. Take two more stitches through all layers. Leave the thread dangling.

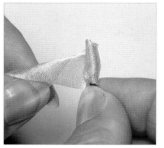

7 **Petals.** Hold the centre in your right hand. Fold the top edge of the ribbon back and down with your other hand.

8 Wrap the folded ribbon once around the centre.

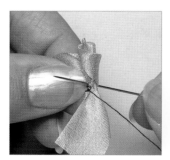

9 Using the dangling thread, take the needle through all layers at the base of the rose.

10 Pull the thread through. Work a second stitch through all layers.

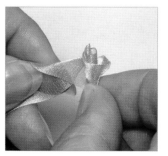

11 Fold the top edge of the ribbon back and down once again.

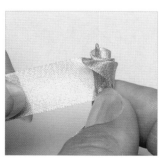

12 Wrap the folded ribbon once around the centre.

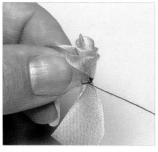

**13** Pulling the thread firmly, work two stitches through all layers at the base of the rose to secure the petal.

**14** Continue folding, wrapping and stitching until the rose is the desired size.

**15** Cut off the excess ribbon leaving a tail that is the width of the ribbon plus 1.5cm (⅝") long. Fold the ribbon back and down as before.

**16** Wrap the ribbon to form a partial petal.

**17 Securing the rose.** Turn the rose upside down. Pulling firmly, take several stitches through the base to secure.

**18** End off the thread.

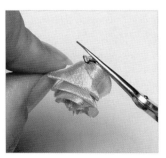

**19** Trim away the tail as close as possible to the base without cutting the stitching.

**20** The rose (worked in 15mm (⅝") metallic ribbon) is now ready to be attached to the fabric.

**21** Folded ribbon rose worked with 7mm (⁵⁄₁₆") silk ribbon.

**22** Folded ribbon roses worked with 12mm (½") rayon ribbon and 20mm (¾") chiffon tubing.

**23** Folded ribbon rose worked with 15mm (⅝") silk ribbon.

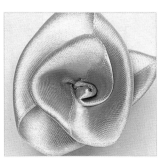

**24** Folded ribbon rose worked with 35mm (1 ⅜") hand dyed satin ribbon.

# FRENCH KNOT

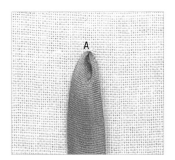

1 Bring the ribbon to the front at A.

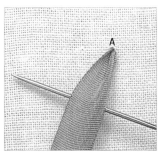

2 Hold the ribbon taut in the left hand. Place the needle under the ribbon approx 1.5cm (⅝") away from A.

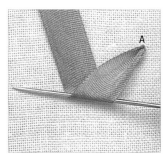

3 Still holding the ribbon taut, take it behind the needle and towards A.

4 Take the ribbon over the needle, forming one wrap.

5 Place the tip of the needle into the fabric very close to A, allowing the wrap to slide down the needle and onto the fabric.

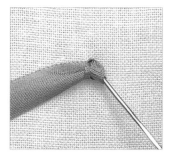

6 Pull the ribbon to tighten the knot slightly. Do not pull it too tight as it will become difficult to pull the needle through.

7 Take the needle to the back and begin to gently pull the ribbon through.

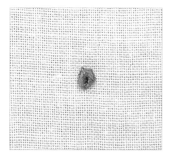

8 Continue pulling until a small knot sits on the fabric. **Completed French knot.**

## Beginning and ending off

It is not advisable to begin ribbon embroidery with a knot as, apart from being bulky, the ribbon knot may become untied over time. Leave a 1.5cm (⅝") tail of ribbon on the back of the fabric. Take the ribbon through to the right side of the fabric, holding the tail on the wrong side. When making the next stitch, ensure it passes through the ribbon tail. Trim away any excess tails of ribbon when the embroidery is complete.

To end off, take the needle and ribbon through to the wrong side. Make a small stitch through an adjacent length of ribbon on the back of the fabric. Make a second stitch close to the first and then cut away the excess length.

Alternatively, secure the tails of ribbon to the back of the fabric with thread. Ensure the stitches are behind embroidered sections so they will not show on the front.

# GATHERED RIBBON BLOSSOM

These beautiful flowers can be made with any number of petals. When dividing the ribbon into evenly spaced sections each section will form one petal–the more sections the more petals and vice versa.

1 Cut a piece of ribbon the required length. Mark the ribbon into evenly spaced intervals.

2 Knot a length of sewing thread. Starting approx 3mm (⅛") from one end, work tiny running stitches until almost at the opposite edge.

3 Turn the corner and work running stitch along the edge until reaching the first mark.

4 Turn the corner again and continue stitching to the opposite edge, ending with the needle on the back.

5 Bring the needle to the front over the fold and continue working running stitch back to the opposite edge.

6 Turn the corner and work running stitch to the second mark.

7 Continue working running stitch in the same manner to the end of the ribbon.

8 Pull up the gathers to form the petals.

9 Place the ends right sides together and stitch. End off the thread.

10 Position the petals on the fabric and attach them with tiny stab stitches around the centre.

11 Fill the centre with a cluster of beads or knots. **Completed blossom.**

# GATHERED RIBBON ROSE

1 Cut a piece of ribbon, long enough to complete the entire rose.

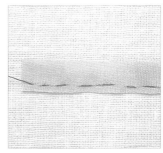

2 Using machine sewing thread with the end knotted, work tiny running stitches along one edge. Leave the thread dangling.

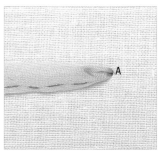

3 Thread one end of the ribbon into a chenille needle. Take the ribbon to the back of the fabric at the centre of the flower (A).

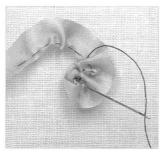

4 Using a new length of machine sewing thread, secure the ribbon on the back of the fabric. Bring the thread to the front close to A.

5 Begin pulling up the gathers close to A and couch the ribbon in place.

6 Continue gathering and couching the ribbon, forming a spiral as you work.

7 When reaching the end of the ribbon, tuck it under. Couch in place and end off the threads on the back. **Completed gathered rose.**

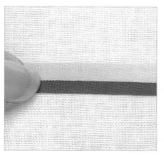

8 To work a two-tone rose, place two ribbons of different widths together so they match along one edge.

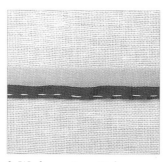

9 Work running stitch through both ribbons close to the edge.

10 Work the rose following steps 2–7. **Completed two-tone gathered rose.**

# GRAB STITCH

Grab stitch makes an effective calyx. It needs to be worked in association with another stitch such as a ribbon stitch or an object such as a folded ribbon rosebud.

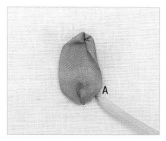

1 Bring the ribbon to the front of the fabric at A, alongside the bud.

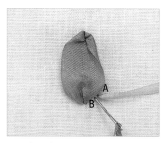

2 Take the needle to the back at B, next to A.

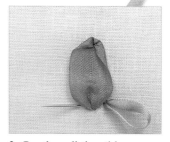

3 Gently pull the ribbon through, leaving a loop on the front.

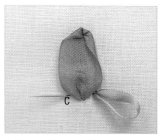

4 Bring the needle to the front at C, on the other side of the bud.

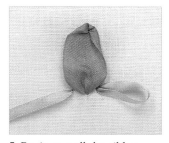

5 Begin to pull the ribbon through, taking care not to shorten the loop.

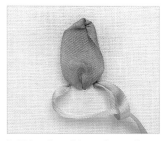

6 Take the ribbon through the loop and begin to pull it gently towards you.

7 Continue pulling until the loop sits snugly around the emerging ribbon and lies across the base of foundation.

8 Take the ribbon to the back at the desired position for the end of the anchoring stitch. **Completed grab stitch.**

# LOOP STITCH

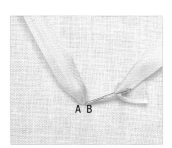

1 Bring the ribbon to the front at A. Spread the ribbon out flat with the needle and take the needle to the back at B, very close to A.

2 Begin to pull the ribbon through, making sure it does not twist.

3 Place a skewer or similar into the loop. Continue pulling the ribbon, tensioning it slightly with the skewer, until the loop is the desired size.

4 Remove the skewer. Secure the ends of the ribbon on the back of the fabric. **Completed loop stitch.**

# LOOP STITCH – BOW

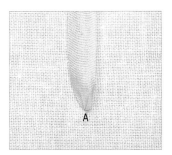

1 Bring the ribbon to the front at A.

2 Spread ribbon out flat with needle and take the needle to the back at B, next to A.

3 Pull the ribbon through until the loop is the desired length.

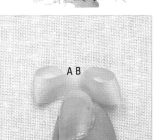

4 Flatten the loop onto the fabric so the centre of the loop lies over A and B.

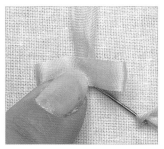

5 Bring the ribbon to the front just above A and B. Take the needle to the back just below A and B.

6 Pull the ribbon through to form a small straight stitch. **Completed bow.**

---

# LOOP STITCH – FLOWER 1

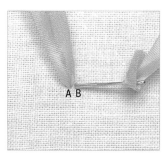

1 **Petals.** Bring the ribbon to the front at A. Spread the ribbon out flat with the needle and take the needle to the back at B, next to A.

2 Pull the ribbon through, making sure it does not twist. Pull until a tiny loop is left on the right side of the fabric.

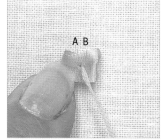

3 Flatten the loop so the centre is over A and B. Holding the loop in place, bring the desired thread to front through centre of loop.

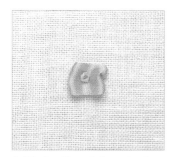

4 Work a French knot in the centre. **Completed loop stitch flower.**

# LOOP STITCH – FLOWER 2

**1** Petals. Mark a tiny circle for the centre of the flower. Bring the ribbon to the front at A.

**2** Spread the ribbon out flat with the needle.

**3** Keeping your thumb or finger on the ribbon, fold it over towards the centre to form a loop.

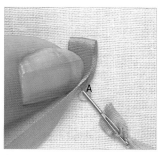

**4** Reposition your thumb or finger to hold both layers of ribbon. Take the needle to the back next to A.

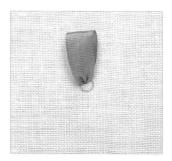

**5** Gently pull the ribbon through until a small loop is formed.

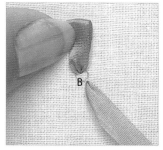

**6** Keeping your thumb over the loop to prevent it pulling through, bring the ribbon to the front at B.

**7** Form a second loop by following steps 2–5.

**8** Keeping your thumb on the second loop, bring the ribbon to the front at C. Form a loop in the same manner.

**9** Repeat the procedure for the desired number of petals.

**10** End off the ribbon and secure each petal on the back of the fabric.

**11** Fill the centre with a colonial knot, French knot or beads. **Completed loop stitch flower.**

# PISTIL STITCH

# PLUME STITCH

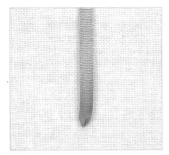

**1** Bring the ribbon to the front at the base of the stitch.

**2** Holding the ribbon taut, take it over the needle.

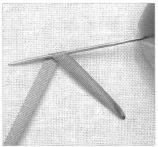

**1** Take the ribbon from A to B. Place a spare needle under the ribbon. Pull the ribbon through, keeping it tensioned with the spare needle.

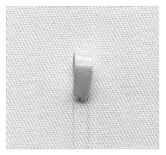

**2** Pull the ribbon through until a loop of the desired size is formed.

**3** Keeping the ribbon taut, wrap it around the needle in an anti-clockwise direction.

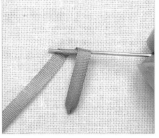

**4** Still keeping the ribbon taut, turn the needle towards the fabric. Place the point into the fabric at the position for the tip of the stitch.

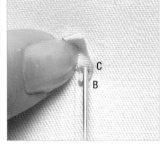

**3** Flatten the loop away from you and hold in place. Bring the needle to the front at C, through the previous stitch just above B.

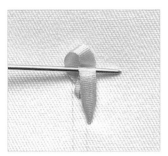

**4** Pull the ribbon through. Work a second stitch in the same manner as the first stitch.

**5** Slide the wraps down the needle onto the fabric. Maintaining tension on the ribbon, push the needle through the fabric.

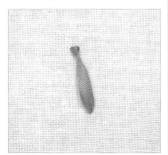

**6** Pull the ribbon all the way through. End off on the back of the fabric. **Completed pistil stitch.**

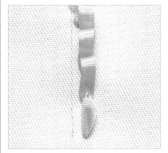

**5** Continue working the required number of stitches. Pull the last stitch flat. End off on the back. **Completed plume stitch.**

# RIBBON FILLER

# RIBBON STITCH

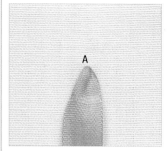

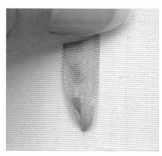

**1** Leaving a tail of approx 1cm (⅜") long, fold the ribbon into a loop of the desired length.

**2** Squeeze the ribbon together at base of loop. Using matching machine sewing thread, secure loop with several stitches at base.

**1** Bring the ribbon to the front at the position for the base of the stitch (A).

**2** Hold the ribbon flat on the fabric with your thumb.

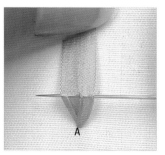

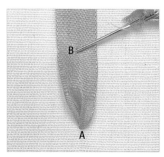

**3** Leave the thread dangling. Fold a second loop of the same length.

**4** Squeeze the ribbon together at the base and attach the second loop to the first with the dangling thread.

**3** Place needle under ribbon near A. Using a slight upward pressure, move needle towards your thumb to smooth and spread ribbon.

**4** Place the tip of the needle in the centre of the ribbon at the position for the tip of the stitch (B).

**5** Leave the thread dangling. Fold a third loop of the same length and attach in the same manner.

**6** End off the thread. Trim the ribbon tails to approx 3mm (⅛"). The ribbon filler is now ready to be attached to the fabric.

**5** Take needle to back of fabric. Place thumb over the stitch to keep it untwisted (thumb not shown). Begin to gently pull ribbon through.

**6** Pull until the ribbon folds back on itself at the tip and the edges curl. **Completed ribbon stitch.**

# RIBBON ROSEBUD

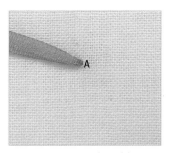

1 **Centre.** Bring the ribbon to the front of the fabric at A.

2 Work a twisted detached chain for the centre of the bud. End off the ribbon on the back of the fabric.

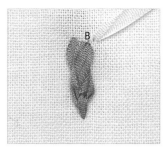

3 **Side petals.** Change to a lighter coloured ribbon. Bring ribbon to front at B, slightly to one side of the base.

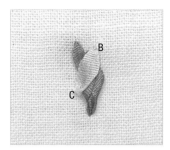

4 Work a ribbon stitch across the bud to C.

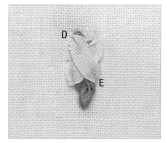

5 Work a second petal from D to E in the same manner.

6 **Sepals.** With green ribbon, work two ribbon stitches in the same manner. Make them slightly shorter than the petals.

7 Change to green thread and work a fly stitch around the base of the bud.

8 Work a straight stitch from base to halfway along bud. Work two straight stitches of different lengths from the tip. **Completed ribbon rosebud.**

# RIBBON STITCH – FOLDED

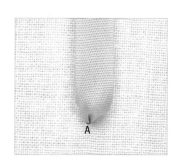

1 Bring the ribbon to the front at the position for the base of the stitch (A).

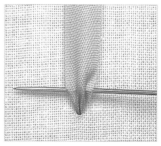

2 Hold ribbon flat on fabric with thumb (thumb not shown). Spread it by moving needle behind while applying a slight upwards pressure.

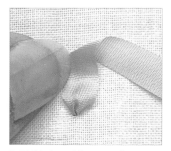

3 Fold the ribbon under a short distance from the base of the stitch.

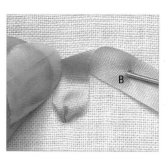

4 Hold the fold in place. Place the tip of the needle in the centre of the ribbon at the position for the tip of the stitch (B).

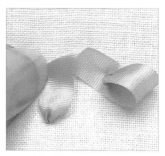

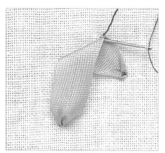

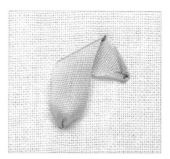

5 Still holding the fold in place, begin to gently pull the ribbon through.

6 Pull until the ribbon folds back on itself at the tip and the edges curl.

7 If desired, couch the ribbon to the fabric at the fold with matching thread.

8 **Completed folded ribbon stitch.**

# RIBBON STITCH – LOOPED

Looping the ribbon before completing a ribbon stitch adds further dimension to your finished embroidery.

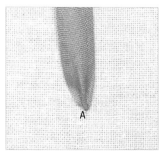

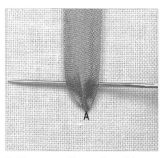

1 Bring the ribbon to the front at the position for the base of the stitch (A).

2 Place needle under ribbon near A. Using a slight upward pressure, move needle towards thumb to spread the ribbon (thumb not shown).

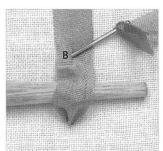

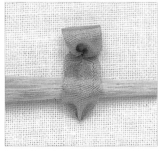

3 Place a chopstick or similar object under the ribbon, close to where it emerged from the fabric.

4 Holding the ribbon over the chopstick, place the tip of the needle at B, in the centre of the ribbon at the position for the tip of the stitch.

5 Still holding the ribbon in place, take the needle to the back of the fabric and begin to gently pull the ribbon through.

6 Pull until the ribbon folds back on itself at the tip and the edges curl. Remove the chopstick. **Completed looped ribbon stitch**.

# RIBBON STITCH – SIDE

S ide ribbon stitch is a variation of ribbon stitch. It creates a stitch that curls to one side depending on the placement of the needle at the tip.

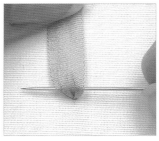

**1** Bring the ribbon to the front at the position for the base of the stitch (A).

**2** Hold the ribbon flat with your thumb. Spread it by moving the needle behind it while applying a slight upward pressure.

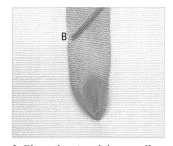

**3** Place the tip of the needle just in from the edge of the ribbon at the position for the end of the stitch (B).

**4** Take needle to back of fabric. Place thumb over the stitch to keep it untwisted (thumb not shown). Begin to gently pull ribbon through.

**5** Pull until the ribbon folds back on itself at the tip and the upper edge curls. **Completed side ribbon stitch.**

**6** By placing the needle on the other side of the ribbon, the tip of the stitch will curl in the opposite direction.

# ROLLED ROSE

P repare a needle threaded with matching machine sewing thread before you begin.

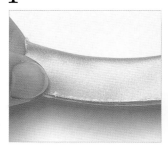

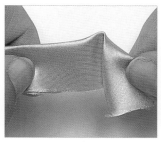

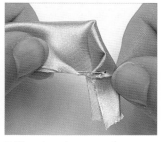

**1** Cut a strip of fabric on the bias or use bias cut ribbon. Fold the ribbon in half along the length.

**2** With the folded edge at the top, fold down one end diagonally so that a tail of approx 1.5cm (⅝") extends below the raw edge.

**3** Keeping the raw edges even, fold over the end. Take 2 or 3 tiny stitches through the base to secure.

**4** Leave the thread dangling. Still keeping the raw edges even, begin to roll the folded end.

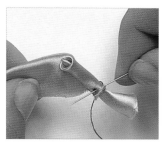

**5** Secure the roll with 2 or 3 tiny stitches through all layers at the base.

**6** Continue rolling and securing until rose is desired size. Cut off excess, leaving a tail the width of the folded ribbon plus 1.5cm (⅝") long.

**7** Diagonally fold the ribbon back and down so a 1.5cm (⅝") tail extends below the lower edge.

**8** Roll diagonal end onto rose. Tightly wrap thread around base 3 or 4 times and secure. Trim tails close to base. **Completed rolled rose.**

# RUNNING STITCH

To achieve flat even stitches, ensure they are always longer than the width of the ribbon you are using.

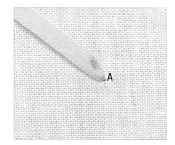

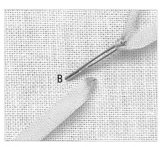

**1** Bring the ribbon to the front at the right hand end of the line (A).

**2** Hold ribbon flat with thumb (thumb not shown). Spread it by moving needle behind it while applying a slight upward pressure.

**3** Take the needle to the back of the fabric at B. Ensure the distance between A and B is longer than the width of the ribbon.

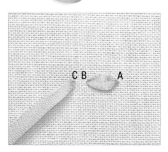

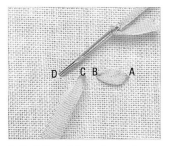

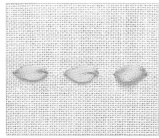

**4** Pull the ribbon through. Re-emerge at C. The distance from B to C is no longer than the distance from A to B.

**5** Pull the ribbon through. Smooth and spread as before. Take the needle to the back at D. C to D is the same distance as A to B.

**6** Pull the ribbon through. Continue working stitches in the same manner for the required distance. **Completed running stitch.**

# RUNNING STITCH – COLONIAL KNOT COMBINATION

A combination of running stitches and a colonial knot are used to create this ingenious rose.

More running stitches can be used to form more petals but it is important to keep them all the same length.

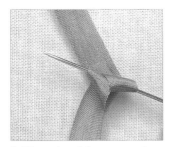

**1** Bring the ribbon to the front of the fabric at A.

**2** Wrap the ribbon around the needle as if making a colonial knot, but approx 5–6cm (2–2 ⅜") from the fabric.

**3** Take 6–8 running stitches, each approx 6mm (¼") long, down the middle of the ribbon.

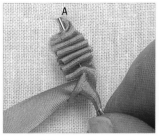

**4** Insert the needle into the fabric close to A. Tighten the knot. Begin to pull the needle through to the back of the fabric.

**5** Continue pulling until the ribbon folds up into petals with a colonial knot in the middle.

**6** End off on the back of the fabric. Adjust the petals with the eye of the needle. Completed rose.

# RUNNING STITCH – WHIPPED

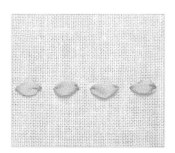

**1 Foundation.** Work a line of running stitch following the instructions on page 27.

**2 Whipping.** Bring the ribbon to the front at the right hand end of the line.

**3** Take the needle from top to bottom under the first running stitch. Do not go through the fabric.

**4** Pull the ribbon through leaving it fairly loose. Allow the ribbon to twist freely.

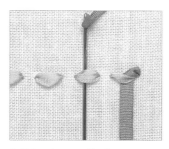  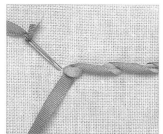 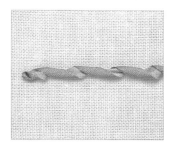

**5** Take the needle from top to bottom behind the second running stitch. Do not go through the fabric.

**6** Pull the ribbon through loosely. Continue to the end of the running stitches in the same manner.

**7** Take the needle to the back of the fabric near the end of the last running stitch.

**8** Pull the ribbon through and end off on the back of the fabric. **Completed whipped running stitch.**

# RUNNING STITCH – DOUBLE WHIPPED

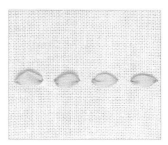 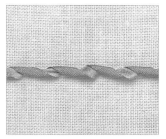 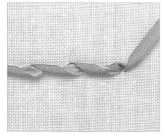 

**1 Foundation.** Work a line of running stitch following the instructions on page 27.

**2 First row of whipping.** Whip the running stitch following the instructions on page 28.

**3 Second row of whipping.** Change to a different ribbon. Bring ribbon to front at right hand end of the line, close to where first ribbon emerged.

**4** Take the needle from top to bottom behind the ribbon only between the first and second running stitches.

   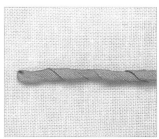

**5** Pull the ribbon through loosely.

**6** Take the needle from top to bottom behind the ribbon between the second and third running stitches. Do not go through the fabric.

**7** Pull the ribbon through loosely. Continue to the end of the line in the same manner.

**8** Take the needle to the back of the fabric near the end of the last running stitch and end off. **Completed double whipped running stitch.**

# SPIDER WEB ROSE

This easy to stitch, textured rose is created by weaving the ribbon through a framework of straight stitch spokes. It is important to always use an uneven number of spokes. Here five spokes are used but when working larger roses more may be required.

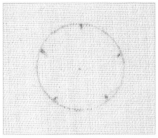

1 Draw a circle and mark the centre with a dot. Imagining the circle is a clock face, mark the outer edge with dots at 12, 2, 5, 7 and 10 o'clock.

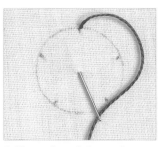

2 Using thread, bring the needle to the front at the 12 o'clock mark. Take it to the back at the centre.

3 Pull the thread through. Work straight stitches from the 5 o'clock and 7 o'clock marks to the centre.

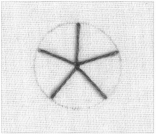

4 Work straight stitches from the 10 o'clock and 2 o'clock marks in the same manner. Secure the thread on the back but leave it dangling.

5 **Petals.** Bring the ribbon to the front between two spokes as close as possible to the centre.

6 Working in an anti-clockwise direction, weave the ribbon over and under the spokes of the framework until one round is complete.

7 Pull the ribbon firmly so the framework does not show at the centre.

8 Work 1 to 2 more rounds in same manner, maintaining the over and under sequence. Take ribbon to back. Secure with dangling thread.

9 Bring a lighter shade of ribbon to the front, emerging next to where the previous ribbon went to the back.

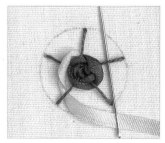

10 Using a looser tension and allowing the ribbon to twist, weave it over and under the spokes.

11 Continue weaving until framework is entirely hidden. Take needle over one more spoke, tuck it under the next spoke and take it to the back.

12 Pull the ribbon through and secure the uncaught tails with the dangling thread. **Completed spider web rose.**

# STEM STITCH

Stem stitch is very similar in appearance to outline stitch and the two are often interchangable. The ribbon is always kept above the needle for outline stitch and below the needle for stem stitch.

# STEM STITCH – TWISTED

Twisting the ribbon in opposite directions achieves different looks. Twisting the ribbon in an anti-clockwise direction will give a row of stitches with a solid appearance. Twisting the ribbon in a clockwise direction will give the stitches a rope-like appearance.

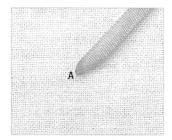

1 Bring the ribbon to the right side of the fabric at A.

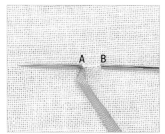

2 Take needle from B to A. With ribbon below needle, hold it flat on the fabric with thumb (thumb not shown).

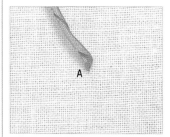

1 Bring the ribbon to the front at A. Twirl needle in a clockwise direction so the ribbon twists.

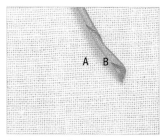

2 Take needle from B to A. With ribbon below needle, hold it against the fabric with thumb (thumb not shown).

3 Still holding the ribbon against the fabric, gently pull the ribbon through.

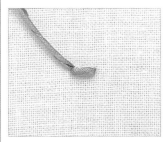

4 Take needle from C to B. Again, position ribbon below the needle and hold it flat on the fabric with your thumb.

3 Still holding the ribbon against the fabric, pull the ribbon through. Twist the ribbon as before.

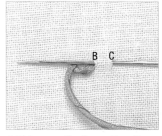

4 Take needle from C to B. Again, position ribbon below the needle and hold it against the fabric with your thumb.

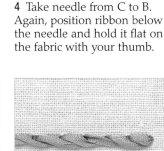

5 Gently pull the ribbon through as before. Continue in the same manner, ensuring the ribbon is untwisted for each stitch.

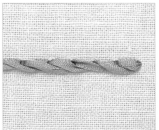

6 For the last stitch, take the needle to the back but do not re-emerge. Pull the ribbon through. **Completed stem stitch.**

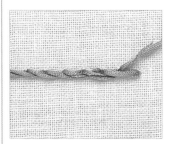

5 Pull the ribbon through as before. Continue in the same manner, ensuring the ribbon is twisted for each stitch.

6 For the last stitch, take the needle to the back but do not re-emerge. Pull the ribbon through. **Completed twisted stem stitch.**

# STEM STITCH – WHIPPED

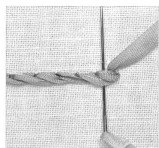

**1** Following the instructions on page 31, work a line of stem stitch to form the foundation for the whipping.

**2** Bring a new length of ribbon to the front of the fabric just above the last stem stitch.

**3** Slide needle from bottom to top behind beginning of first stem stitch from the right and end of second stitch. Do not go through fabric.

**4** Ensure the ribbon is flat and untwisted. Pull the ribbon through.

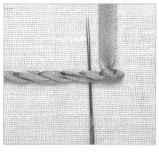

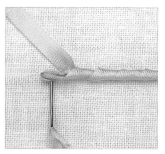

**5** Slide needle as before going behind beginning of second stem stitch from the right and end of third stitch. Do not go through the fabric.

**6** Ensure the ribbon is flat and untwisted. Pull the ribbon through.

**7** Continue in the same manner to the end of the row. To end off, take the needle to the back of the fabric behind the last stem stitch.

**8** End off on the back of the fabric. **Completed whipped stem stitch.**

## Care of ribbon embroidery

### Cleaning

It is important to test ribbons before washing as some are not colourfast, particularly hand dyed and strong coloured ribbons.

To clean, gently wash the item by hand using luke warm water and mild detergent. Rinse well and gently squeeze out the moisture. Place the piece right side up over a board (eg a quilter's pressing board) and stretch to shape. Allow to dry.

### Framing

Choose a professional framer who is familiar with ribbon embroidered pieces. To prevent the glass touching the embroidery, it is best to select a box type framing method. As the ribbons are subject to fading in direct sunlight or strong artificial light, use conservation glass to screen out harmful UV rays.

# STRAIGHT STITCH

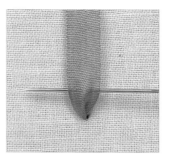

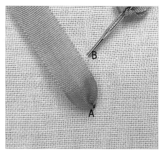

**1** Bring the ribbon to the front of the fabric at A.

**2** Hold ribbon flat on fabric with thumb. Smooth and spread it by moving needle behind it while applying a slight upward pressure.

**3** Ensuring the ribbon remains flat, take the needle to the back at B, the required distance away.

**4** Gently pull the ribbon through, keeping it untwisted. **Completed straight stitch.**

# STRAIGHT STITCH – LOOPED

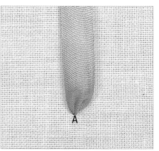

**1** Bring the ribbon to the front of the fabric at A.

**2** Hold ribbon flat on fabric with thumb. Smooth and spread it by moving needle behind it while applying a slight upward pressure.

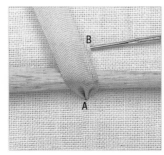

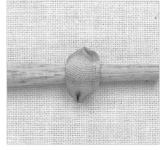

**3** Place a chopstick or similar object under the ribbon, close to where it emerged from the fabric.

**4** Holding the ribbon over the chopstick, take the needle to the back of the fabric at B, the required distance away.

**5** Gently pull the ribbon through, keeping it untwisted.

**6** End off on the back of the fabric. **Completed looped straight stitch.**

# STRAIGHT STITCH – PADDED

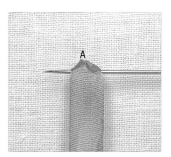

**1** Bring ribbon to front at A. Hold flat on fabric with thumb. Spread it by moving needle behind it while applying a slight upward pressure.

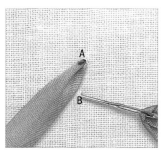

**2** Ensuring the ribbon remains flat, take the needle to the back at B, the required distance away.

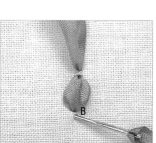

**3** Gently pull the ribbon through. Bring the needle to the front just above A.

**4** Pull the ribbon through and smooth as before. Take the needle to the back just below B.

**5** Gently pull ribbon through, covering previous stitch. Bring needle to front just beyond the beginning of the second stitch.

**6** Pull ribbon through and smooth as before. Take needle to back just below end of previous stitch. **Completed padded straight stitch.**

# STRAIGHT STITCH – TWISTED

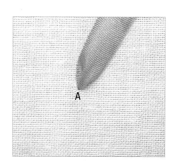

**1** Bring the ribbon to the front of the fabric at A.

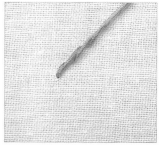

**2** Holding the ribbon taut, roll the needle between your thumb and forefinger until the ribbon is tightly twisted.

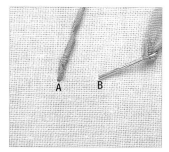

**3** Keeping tension on the ribbon so it does not unravel, take the needle to the back at B.

**4** Still maintaining tension on ribbon, gently pull it through until it lies snug against fabric. **Completed twisted straight stitch.**

# STRAIGHT STITCH – WHIPPED

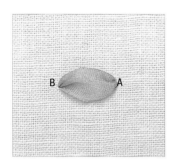

1 Work a straight stitch from A to B, following the instructions on page 33.

2 Bring the ribbon to the front just below and to the left of A.

3 Take the needle from top to bottom under the straight stitch. Do not go through the fabric.

4 Ensuring the ribbon does not twist, pull it through until it snugly wraps around the straight stitch.

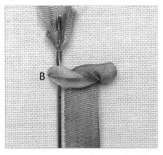

5 Moving towards B, take the needle from top to bottom under the straight stitch again.

6 Pull the ribbon through to form a second wrap that slightly overlaps the first wrap.

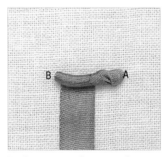

7 Continue whipping the straight stitch until reaching B. Ensure the ribbon is smooth and the stitches slightly overlap.

8 Take the needle to the back of the fabric under the straight stitch. **Completed whipped straight stitch.**

## Storing ribbons

Silk ribbons should be stored so that no sharp creases are formed. They are best wound onto cardboard or plastic cylinders, or even rolled up cards that have first been covered with acid free paper. Cut a slit in each end of the cylinder to ensure the ends of the ribbon are anchored securely.

Sort the ribbons into colour ranges and store away from direct sunlight.

If you find that your ribbons have formed creases, you may need to press them. Set the iron at the appropriate setting. Lay the iron onto the ironing board and slowly pull the ribbon between the iron and the board (*see diag*).

# TWIRLED RIBBON ROSE

Use a short length of ribbon, no longer than 20cm (8"), so the ribbon does not become worn.

**1** Secure the ribbon on the back of the fabric. Bring it to the front at the position for the centre of the rose (A).

**2** Hold the needle up so that the ribbon is vertical to the fabric. Begin to twist the needle in an anti-clockwise direction.

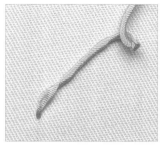

**3** Continue twirling the needle until the ribbon is tightly twisted. Stop when the ribbon begins to buckle.

**4** Using your thumb and forefinger, hold the coiled ribbon approx 3cm (1 ¼") from the fabric.

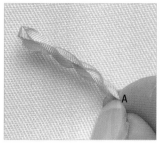

**5** Keeping the ribbon taut, fold it over to form a loop.

**6** Hold the two parts of the ribbon close to A. Release the looped end. The ribbon will twist around itself forming a double coil.

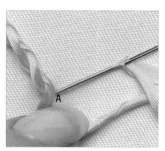

**7** Still holding the double coil, take the needle to the back of the fabric just next to A.

**8** Pull the ribbon through until reaching the doubled coil. Continue pulling gently until the rose is the desired size.

**9** Using matching sewing thread, secure with two tiny stitches through the ribbon near the centre. Place stitches as invisibly as possible.

**10 Completed twirled ribbon rose.**

# The designs

# DAFFODILS

by Helen Eriksson

## This design uses

*Couching, Folded ribbon stitch, French knot, Looped ribbon stitch, Pistil stitch, Ribbon stitch, Straight stitch, Twisted straight stitch*

### Ribbon embroidery index

Couching 11
Folded ribbon stitch 24
Looped ribbon stitch 25
Ribbon stitch 23
Straight stitch 33
Twisted straight stitch 34

## Materials

### Threads & ribbons

*Anchor stranded cotton*
A = 267 dk avocado green
*Anchor Marlitt stranded rayon*
B = 868 old gold
*Hanah hand dyed bias cut silk ribbon 11mm (⁷⁄₁₆") wide*
C = 2m (2yd 7") mossy rock
*YLI silk ribbon 2mm (⅛") wide*
D = 1m (39 ½") no. 21 dk forest green
*YLI silk ribbon 4mm (³⁄₁₆") wide*
E = 1m (39 ½") no. 15 bright yellow
F = 1m (39 ½") no. 20 forest green
G = 1.5m (1yd 23") no. 54 old gold
H = 3m (3yd 10") no. 72 dk olive green
*YLI silk ribbon 7mm (⁵⁄₁₆") wide*
I = 3m (3yd 10") no. 13 vy lt yellow
J = 2m (2yd 7") no. 15 bright yellow
K = 1m (39 ½") no. 20 forest green
L = 1.5m (1yd 23") no. 54 old gold
M = 1m (39 ½") no. 72 dk olive green

### Needles

No. 5 straw (milliner's) needle
No. 18 chenille needle
No. 20 chenille needle

## Order of work

Refer to the photograph as a guide for colour changes within the design.

Use the no. 20 chenille needle for the 4mm (³⁄₁₆") ribbon and the no. 18 chenille needle for the 7mm (⁵⁄₁₆") ribbon. Use the straw needle for all thread embroidery.

### Front view daffodils

Work the flowers and stems following the step-by-step instructions. There are four pale daffodils and three dark daffodils. Omit the calyx for some of the blooms.

### Side view daffodils

Embroider three daffodils in a similar manner to the front view daffodils, stitching the flower on the lower right hand side with only five petals. Work the frilled edge of the trumpet as a row and not an oval and omit the pistil stitches.

### Back view daffodil

Work a single daffodil and stem at the top of the design with six petals radiating from the centre. Add the calyx with six tiny ribbon stitches.

### Buds

Embroider five buds around the outer edge. Stitch the petals with two slightly overlapping ribbon stitches and add a third petal to the bud on the lower left hand side. Stitch the calyx with two or three loose ribbon stitches that cup the bud. Work the stems next.

### Leaves

Scatter long ribbon stitch leaves among the daffodils, adding a fold to some of the leaves. Take several leaves behind the stems. Embroider a straight stitch at the base on some of the leaves for the vein.

### Grass

Add three clumps of grass at the base of the stems and leaves, making a fold or twist in a few of the blades.

## Embroidery key

*All thread embroidery is worked with one strand.*

### Front view daffodils

Petals = I or J (ribbon stitch)
Trumpet = J or L (ribbon stitch)
Trumpet frill = E or G (looped ribbon stitch)
Stamens = B (French knot, 1–2 wraps, pistil stitch, 1 wrap)
Calyx = F or H (ribbon stitch) or none

### Side view daffodils

Petals = I (ribbon stitch)
Trumpet = L (ribbon stitch)
Trumpet frill = G (looped ribbon stitch)
Calyx = H (ribbon stitch) or none

### Back view daffodil

Petals = I (ribbon stitch)
Calyx = H (ribbon stitch)

### Buds

Petals = J or L (ribbon stitch)
Calyx = C or F (ribbon stitch)

*Stems* = F or H (twisted straight stitch, couching)

*Leaves* = C, K or M (ribbon stitch, folded ribbon stitch), A (straight stitch, couching)

*Grass* = D (folded ribbon stitch, straight stitch)

# FRONT VIEW DAFFODIL

1 **Petals.** Mark the position of the entry and exit points for the ribbon on the right side of the fabric.

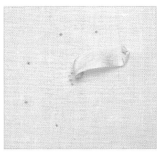

2 Using 7mm (⁵⁄₁₆") ribbon, bring it to the front at the centre point. Work the first petal in loose ribbon stitch.

3 Repeat for five more petals.

4 **Trumpet.** Change ribbon colour. Bring it to the front at centre of petals. Work a ribbon stitch approx 17mm (⁵⁄₈") long.

5 Work a second ribbon stitch slightly overlapping the first and widening at the end.

6 **Frilled edge.** Using a fabric marker, draw an oval shape with its lowest edge just above the end of the trumpet.

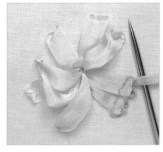

7 Bring the 4mm (³⁄₁₆") ribbon to the front on the oval. Lay the ribbon outwards over a darning needle.

8 Complete the ribbon stitch, ensuring you do not lose the loop in the ribbon.

9 Work approx 12–15 ribbon stitches to cover the oval shape.

10 **Stamens.** Using one strand of thread, stitch French knots and pistil stitches in the centre of the trumpet.

11 **Calyx.** Beginning at the centre of the petals, work two ribbon stitches close together.

12 **Stem.** Bring the ribbon to the front at the end of the calyx. Twist ribbon and take to the back at the base. Couch in place.
**Completed daffodil.**

# DWARF CALLA LILY

## by Helen Eriksson

## Order of work

Use the no. 20 chenille needle for the 4mm (³⁄₁₆") ribbon and the no. 18 chenille needle for the remaining ribbons. Use the straw needle for working all thread embroidery.

### Lilies

Work the lilies in a clump using one ribbon stitch for each flower. Place the stitches in different directions. Add a bullion knot in the centre of each one for the stamen.

### Buds

Work the two buds at the top of the design with a straight stitch. Add a small straight stitch on each side of the bud for the sepals.

### Leaves

Stitch the leaves with ribbon stitch, using the three shades of green ribbon.

### Stems

Stitch the ribbon stems for the flowers and buds with straight stitches, twisting the ribbon tightly. Work the stems for the leaves using stranded cotton.

## This design uses

*Bullion knot, Grab stitch, Ribbon stitch, Straight stitch, Twisted straight stitch*

### Ribbon embroidery index

Ribbon stitch 23
Straight stitch 33
Twisted straight stitch 34

## Materials

### Threads & ribbons

*Anchor stranded cotton*
A = 262 dk pine green
B = 303 pumpkin
*YLI silk ribbon 13mm (½") wide*
C = 50cm (20") no. 3 white
*YLI silk ribbon 7mm (⁵⁄₁₆") wide*
D = 50cm (20") no. 21 dk forest green
E = 50cm (20") no. 32 med grey-green
F = 20cm (8") no. 33 grey-green
*YLI silk ribbon 4mm (³⁄₁₆") wide*
G = 40cm (16") no. 72 dk olive green

### Needles

No. 5 straw (milliner's) needle
No. 18 chenille needle
No. 20 chenille needle

## Embroidery key

*All thread embroidery is worked with two strands.*

### Flowers

Petals = C (ribbon stitch)
Stamens = B (bullion knot, 8–10 wraps)
Stems = G (twisted straight stitch)

### Buds

Petals = C (straight stitch)
Sepals = G (straight stitch)
Stems = G (twisted straight stitch)

### Foliage

Leaves = D, E and F (ribbon stitch)
Stems = A (grab stitch)

# CHERUB CIRCLET

## by Carolyn Pearce

### This design uses

*Colonial knot, Detached chain, Fly stitch, French knot, Loop stitch, Raised stem stitch, Ribbon stitch, Running stitch – colonial knot combination, Smocker's knot, Spider web rose, Stem stitch, Straight stitch, Twirled ribbon rose, Twisted detached chain, Twisted stem stitch*

### Ribbon embroidery index

Colonial knot 9
Loop stitch 19
Ribbon stitch 23
Ribbon rosebud 24
Running stitch – colonial knot combination 28
Spider web rose 30
Stem stitch 31
Stem stitch rose 99
Twirled ribbon rose 36
Twisted detached chain 13
Twisted stem stitch 31

## Materials

*Threads & Ribbons*

*Au Ver à Soie, Soie d'Alger*
A = 3332 lt purple grape
B = 3423 med silver-green
C = 4140 ice blue
D = F19 chicken soup
*The Thread Gatherer's Silk 'n Colours stranded silk*
E = maidenhair fern
*YLI silk floss*
F = 13 shrimp pink
*YLI silk ribbon 4mm (³⁄₁₆") wide*
G = 1m (39 ½") no. 12 ultra lt yellow
H = 2m (2yd 7") no. 158 dk dusky pink
I = 1m (39 ½") no. 163 med dusky pink
*Colour Streams hand dyed silk ribbon 4mm (³⁄₁₆") wide*
J = 3.5m (3yd 30") antique rose
*Glen Lorin hand dyed silk ribbon 4mm (³⁄₁₆") wide*
K = 1.5m (1yd 23") mountain green
*The Thread Gatherer's Silken Ribbons silk ribbon 4mm (³⁄₁₆") wide*
L = 1.5m (1yd 23") heirloom blue

### Needles

No. 10 crewel needle
No. 13 chenille needle
No. 22 chenille needle
No. 26 tapestry needle

### Supplies

2cm (¾") high cherub
Craft glue

## Order of work

Use the photograph as a guide for ribbon and thread colour changes within the design.

Use the no. 22 chenille needle for all ribbon embroidery and the no. 13 chenille needle for forming the ribbon loops. The tapestry needle is used for working the raised stem stitch and the crewel needle is used for all other thread embroidery.

### Ribbon band

Work the framework for the raised stem stitch with straight stitches approximately 2mm (⅛") apart. Embroider the raised stem stitch, keeping the rows packed firmly together.

### Large roses

Embroider the five stem stitch roses, stitching seven colonial knots for the centre and four or five stem stitches for the inner round of petals. When working the outer round, put a twist in the ribbon as you take each stitch. Guide the stitch into place by putting a spare needle under the ribbon to help maintain the twist.

### Medium roses

In the upper right hand corner of the design, embroider a spider web rose, a twirled ribbon rose and a stem stitch rose in a cluster below the large roses. Use a single colonial knot for the centre of the stem stitch rose.

Stitch a spider web rose alongside the large rose in the lower right corner and then a twirled rose and a stem stitch rose near the large rose in the lower left hand corner.

### Small roses

Work three running stitch – colonial knot combination roses in the lower half of the design.

### Blue flowers

Embroider a colonial knot for the centre of each flower. Work five loop stitches for the petals. Place the no. 13 chenille needle in each loop as you pull the ribbon through so all loops will be the same size.

Stitch a pair of ribbon stitch leaves near most of the flowers.

### Rosebuds

Embroider the thirteen rosebuds around the design, singly and in pairs, following the step-by-step instructions.

### Large leaves

Embroider the fly stitch leaves using the silver green and the maidenhair fern threads. Finish each leaf with a smocker's knot worked at the base.

### Mauve forget-me-nots

Work a single colonial knot for the centre and then five colonial knots for the petals.

Add pairs and trios of detached chain leaves close to some of the forget-me-nots. Use a long anchoring stitch on each detached chain to give the leaves a pointed appearance.

### Pink sprays

Stitch the base of each spray with three to seven colonial knots in a loose cluster. Change to French knots and gradually taper to a single knot at the tip of each one.

### Cherub

Squeeze a small amount of glue onto the back of the cherub. Spread the glue out to the edges with a toothpick. Firmly press the cherub onto the fabric and hold down firmly for several minutes. Leave to dry.

## Embroidery key

*All thread embroidery is worked with one strand unless otherwise specified.*

*Ribbon band* = C (raised stem stitch)

### Large roses

Centre = H (colonial knot)
Petals = I (stem stitch), J (twisted stem stitch)

*Medium roses* = J (spider web rose, twirled ribbon rose, stem stitch, colonial knot)

*Small roses* = J (running stitch – colonial knot combination)

### Blue flowers

Centre = G (colonial knot)
Petals = L (loop stitch)
Leaves = K (ribbon stitch)

### Rosebuds

Centre = H (twisted detached chain)
Petals = J (ribbon stitch)
Tip = B (straight stitch)
Calyx = K (ribbon stitch), B (fly stitch, straight stitch)

*Large leaves* = B and E (fly stitch, smocker's knot)

### Mauve forget-me-nots

Petals = A (colonial knot)
Centre = D (colonial knot)
Leaves = B (detached chain)

*Pink sprays* = F (3 strands, colonial knot, French knot, 1 wrap)

# VIOLETS

## by Cathy Veide

### This design uses

*French knot, Looped ribbon stitch,*
*Looped straight stitch, Ribbon stitch,*
*Stem stitch, Straight stitch*

### Ribbon embroidery index

Looped ribbon stitch 25
Looped straight stitch 33
Ribbon stitch 23
Straight stitch 33

## Materials

### Threads & ribbons

*DMC stranded cotton*
A = 725 dk golden yellow
B = 3363 med pine green
*Bucilla variegated silk ribbon 13mm*
*(½") wide*
C = 20cm (8") no. 2-1311 olive greens
*YLI silk ribbon 4mm (³⁄₁₆") wide*
D = 50cm (20") no. 118 dk hyacinth
E = 10cm (4") no. 20 forest green

### Needles

No. 8 crewel needle
No. 20 chenille needle
No. 24 chenille needle
Tapestry needle

### Order of work

Use the no. 20 chenille needle for the
13mm (½") ribbons, and the no. 24
chenille needle for the 4mm (³⁄₁₆")
ribbon. Work all thread embroidery with
the crewel needle. The tapestry needle is
used for shaping the leaves.

### Stems and leaves

Begin by embroidering the stems with
stem stitch. Work a looped straight stitch
for each leaf, forming it into an oval
shape with a tapestry needle. Stitch
three radiating straight stitches from the
back towards the tip, to anchor the
centre of each leaf and create the
leaf veins.

### Flowers and bud

For the bud, work a small straight stitch
for the padding. Re-emerge at the tip
and cover the padding with a ribbon
stitch. Place a green straight stitch across
the base for the calyx.

To create each flower, work the upper
petals and centre lower petal with
looped straight stitches. Embroider a
looped ribbon stitch on each side of the
centre lower petal. Add a French knot to
the centre of each flower.

### Embroidery key

*All thread embroidery is worked with
one strand unless otherwise specified.*

#### Flowers

Upper petals & centre lower petal =
D (looped straight stitch)
Side lower petals = D (looped
ribbon stitch)
Centre = A (2 strands, French knot,
2 wraps)

#### Bud

Padding = D (straight stitch)
Petal = D (ribbon stitch)
Calyx = E (straight stitch)

#### Stems and leaves

Stems = B (2 strands, stem stitch)
Leaves = C (looped straight stitch)
Leaf veins = B (straight stitch)

# AQUILEGIAS

## by Helen Eriksson

## Materials

### Thread & ribbons

*Anchor stranded cotton*
A = 268 vy dk avocado green
*YLI silk ribbon 4mm (³⁄₁₆") wide*
B = 20cm (8") no. 13 vy lt yellow
C = 30cm (12") no. 14 lt yellow
D = 30cm (12") no. 15 bright yellow
E = 50cm (20") no. 21 forest green
F = 40cm (16") no. 23 med lavender
G = 30cm (12") no. 54 old gold
H = 50cm (20") no. 72 dk olive green
I = 20cm (8") no. 101 blue-violet

J = 90cm (36") no. 171 avocado green
*Kacoonda hand dyed silk ribbon 4mm (³⁄₁₆") wide*
K = 40cm (16") no. 3C hydrangea
L = 50cm (20") no. 6F coral rose

### Needles

No. 8 crewel needle
No. 20 chenille needle
No. 22 chenille needle

## Order of work

Refer to the photograph as a guide for colour changes within the design.

Use the crewel needle when working the thread embroidery, the no. 22 chenille needle when creating the flower tendrils and the no. 20 chenille needle for all remaining ribbon embroidery.

### Flowers

Work the large flowers first. Stitch four inner petals and then five outer petals. The outer petals don't quite cover the inner petals. To work the tendrils, bring a short length of ribbon to the front at the base of the flower and twist the ribbon tightly until it starts to curl. Take the ribbon to the back at the marked point leaving a twist on the front.

### Buds

Embroider the buds in a similar manner to the flowers, stitching one or two inner petals and two or three outer petals.

### Stems and leaves

Stitch the flower stems in stem stitch. Work a small fly stitch around the base of each bud and then continue working the stem in stem stitch. Embroider the leaves in closely worked ribbon stitch. Add the leaf stems in stem stitch.

## Embroidery key

*All thread embroidery is worked with one strand.*

### Flowers

Inner petals = B, D or G (ribbon stitch)
Outer petals = F, I, K or L (ribbon stitch)
Tendrils = D, F, G, K or L (twisted straight stitch)

### Buds

Inner petals = C or G (ribbon stitch)
Outer petals = I and K, or L (ribbon stitch)
Tendrils = G or L (twisted straight stitch)
Bud calyxes = A (fly stitch)

### Stems and leaves

Stems = A (stem stitch)
Leaves = E, H or J (ribbon stitch)

# AUTUMN GARLAND

## by Beverley Gogel

**This design uses**

*Beading, Bullion knot, Colonial knot,
Detached chain, French knot, Grab stitch,
Looped straight stitch, Pistil stitch,
Straight stitch*

**Ribbon embroidery index**

Colonial knot 9
Detached chain 12
Looped straight stitch 33
Looped straight stitch flower 48
Straight stitch 33

## Materials

### Threads, ribbons & beads

*DMC stranded cotton*
A = 731 dk olive green
B = 732 olive green
C = 733 med olive green
D = 739 ultra lt tan
*DMC stranded rayon*
E = 30739 vanilla
*Anchor Marlitt stranded rayon*
F = 826 med olive
G = 1011 lt olive
*Kacoonda hand dyed thick silk*
H = 106 antique green
*YLI silk ribbon 4mm (³⁄₁₆") wide*
I = 1m (39 ½") no. 56 med olive green
J = 1m (39 ½") no. 171 avocado green
*YLI silk ribbon 7mm (⁵⁄₁₆") wide*
K = 2m (2yd 7") no. 35 honey
*Kacoonda hand dyed silk ribbon 7mm (⁵⁄₁₆") wide*
L = 60cm (24") no. 106 antique green
*Maria George Delica Beads*
M = DBR 456 galvanized olive

### Needles

No. 1 straw (milliner's) needle
No. 7 straw (milliner's) needle
No. 20 chenille needle
Fine beading needle

## Order of work

Use the chenille needle for all ribbon embroidery and the beading needle for attaching the beads. The no. 1 straw needle is used when working with six strands of thread and the no. 7 straw needle for all other thread embroidery.

### Large flowers and buds

Stitch the flowers following the step-by-step instructions. Work a single straight stitch for each bud.

### Pairs of bullion buds

Embroider a pair of bullion knots close to each large flower. Begin the second knot part way along the first. Work a straight stitch between each bullion knot. For the calyx and stem work a grab stitch with a long anchoring stitch at the base of each bud.

### Small cream buds

Work a pair of cream buds close to the outer bullion knots. In each pair, work one knot with the stranded rayon and one with the stranded cotton.

### Foliage

Stitch a pair of detached chain leaves on each side of the large flowers. Use the olive green ribbon for one leaf and the avocado green ribbon for the other leaf in each pair.

Embroider the trios of large knots near the ends of the bullion buds. Add two pairs of knots inside the garland. Using blended threads, add the calyxes to all the buds by working a grab stitch around the base and straight stitches alongside them. Repeat for each detached chain leaf.

Stitch a pair of pistil stitches from each large flower. Scatter small French knots around the outer edge of the garland.

## Embroidery key

*All thread embroidery is worked with one strand unless otherwise specified.*

### Large flowers

Petals = K (looped straight stitch)
Centre = B blended with C (1 strand of each, French knot, 2 wraps), M (beading)
Bud = K (straight stitch)
Bud calyx = B blended with C (1 strand of each, straight stitch, grab stitch)

### Bullion buds

Petals = D (6 strands, bullion knot, 12–14 wraps)
Calyx = B blended with C (1 strand of each, straight stitch, grab stitch)

### Small cream buds

Petals = E or F (6 strands, colonial knot)
Calyx = B blended with C (1 strand of each, grab stitch)

Leaves = I or J (detached chain), B blended with C (1 strand of each, grab stitch, straight stitch)

*Trios of green buds* = L (colonial knot), 6 strands of G blended with 1 strand of H (colonial knot), A, B and C blended together (1 strand of each, French knot, 3 wraps)

*Buds inside circlet* = G (2 strands, French knot, 2 wraps), H (2 strands, French knot, 2 wraps)

*Tiny buds around outer edge* = B blended with C (1 strand of each, pistil stitch, French knot, 1 wrap)

*Vanity Fair*

# LOOPED STRAIGHT STITCH FLOWER

I f you wish to keep the stitches the same height, work them over a cylindrical object such as a chopstick, skewer, finger or large needle. Here we have used a chopstick.

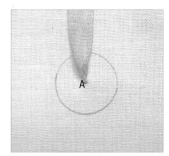

1 Bring the ribbon to the front at A, approx 1.5mm (¹⁄₁₆") from the centre mark. Lay the ribbon flat against the fabric.

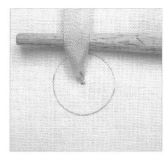

2 Place the chopstick under the ribbon close to where it emerged from the fabric.

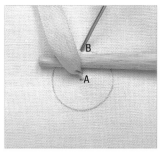

3 Holding the ribbon on the chopstick, take the needle to the back of the fabric at B.

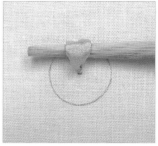

4 Continuing to hold the ribbon in place, carefully pull it through. Ensure there are no twists in the ribbon.

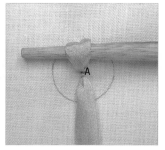

5 Before removing the chopstick, bring the ribbon to the front 1.5mm (¹⁄₁₆") away from the centre, directly opposite A.

6 Remove the chopstick. Following steps 2–4, work a second stitch directly opposite the first.

7 Work a stitch in the same manner, halfway between the previous stitches.

8 Work a stitch directly opposite this stitch.

9 Work four more stitches, placing them between the previous stitches.

10 Add a single bead and two French knots to the centre. **Completed looped straight stitch flower.**

# FORGET-ME-NOTS

## by Angela Dower

### This design uses

*Couching, Fly stitch, Folded ribbon stitch, French knot, Stem stitch, Straight stitch*

### Ribbon embroidery index

## Materials

### Threads & ribbons

*Rajmahal Art silk*
A = 25 Lagerfeld ink
*YLI silk floss*
B = 157 drab olive
*Kacoonda hand dyed fine silk thread*
C = 8E lt olive
*DMC stranded cotton*
D = 745 vy lt yellow
*Glen Lorin hand dyed silk ribbon 4mm (³⁄₁₆") wide*
E = 80cm (31 ½") angel baby
*Kacoonda hand dyed silk ribbon 4mm (³⁄₁₆") wide*
F = 40cm (16") no. 8E lt olive
*YLI silk ribbon 4mm (³⁄₁₆") wide*
G = 20cm (8") no. 22 lavender

### Needles

No. 9 crewel needle
No. 22 chenille needle

## Order of work

Use the crewel needle for all thread embroidery and the chenille needle for all ribbon embroidery.

### Forget-me-nots

Stitch the stems first. Embroider the petals of the four facing and three side view flowers with radiating straight stitches. Add a centre to the full blooms and the lower side view flower.

Using the same ribbon work two overlapping straight stitches for the largest bud. Stitch a tiny straight stitch for the remaining blue buds. At the tip of each stem, add four straight stitches for the remaining buds. Use the olive green ribbon for two of the buds and the lavender for the other two.

Encase each bud with a fly stitch to form the calyx. Use the anchoring stitch to link the bud to the nearest main stem.

Embroider the spent flower heads in a similar manner to the buds, extending the 'arms' of the fly stitch beyond the ribbon and adding one or two straight stitches to the tip.

Work the three leaves in folded ribbon stitch, couching the ribbon at the edge of the fold.

## Embroidery key

*All thread embroidery is worked with one strand.*

### Facing flowers

Petals = E (straight stitch)
Centre = D (straight stitch), A (French knot, 1 wrap)

### Side view flowers

Petals = E (straight stitch)
Centre = D (straight stitch), A (French knot, 1 wrap) or none
Calyx = C (fly stitch, straight stitch) or none

**Spent flower heads** = F (straight stitch), B (fly stitch, straight stitch)

### Buds

Petals = E, F or G (straight stitch)
Calyx = B (fly stitch)

### Stems and leaves

Stems = C (stem stitch)
Leaves = F (folded ribbon stitch), C (couching)

# BASKET OF ROSES

## by Lynda Maker

### This design uses

*Beading, Chain stitch, Gathered ribbon rose,
French knot, Looped ribbon stitch,
Ribbon stitch, Side ribbon stitch,
Split back stitch, Whipping,
Woven filling stitch*

### Ribbon Embroidery Index

Gathered ribbon rose 18
Looped ribbon stitch 25
Padded rosebud 94
Ribbon stitch 23
Side ribbon stitch 26

## Materials

### Threads, ribbons & beads

*Gumnut Yarns 'Stars' stranded silk*
A = 645 med khaki
*Madeira stranded silk*
B = 2209 med old gold
*Waterlilies by Caron 12 ply silk thread*
C = 099 cocoa
*Kacoonda hand dyed silk ribbon 7mm
(⁵⁄₁₆") wide*
D = 1.5m (1yd 23") no. 8J lt fern green
E = 1.5m (1yd 23") no. 306
autumn green
F = 3.5m (3yd 30") no. 310 dusky
rose pink
*Mill Hill glass seed beads*
G = 00275 coral
*Mill Hill antique glass beads*
H = 03056 antique red
*Pearl beads 4mm (³⁄₁₆") in diameter*
I = cream (9 beads)

### Needles

No. 10 crewel needle
No. 18 chenille needle
No. 18 tapestry needle
Fine beading needle

## Order of work

Use the tapestry needle for working the woven filling stitch and the whipping. The chenille needle is used for the ribbon embroidery. Attach the beads with the beading needle and use the crewel needle for all other embroidery.

### Basket

Using the brown silk thread, work sixteen evenly spaced vertical straight stitches and fill with woven filling stitch. Work a row of whipping along the lower edge of the basket over the first row of weaving. Embroider the handle in chain stitch using the same thread as the basket.

### Roses

Make ten gathered roses, using a 25cm (10") length of ribbon for each one. Work clusters of tightly packed French knots for the centres.

### Rosebuds

Stitch the pearl beads in position for the buds around the outer edge of the roses. Embroider one or two ribbon stitches over each bead. Using the green silk ribbon, work a ribbon stitch each side of the bud for the calyx.

### Leaves

Embroider groups of ribbon stitch and side ribbon stitch leaves around the outer area of the design. Fill any remaining spaces around the roses and the basket with leaves worked in looped ribbon stitch, loosely worked ribbon stitch or side ribbon stitch.

### Outer stems and beads

Using the green thread, work the outer stems in split back stitch. Stitch a tiny bead at the end of each stem. Randomly add more beads around the outer edge of the design.

## Embroidery key

*All thread embroidery is worked with one strand unless otherwise specified.*

### Basket

Basket = C (12 strands, woven filling stitch, whipping)
Handle = C (12 strands, chain stitch)

### Roses

Petals = F (gathered ribbon rose)
Centre = B (2 strands, French knot, 1–2 wraps)

### Rosebuds

Petals = F and I (ribbon stitch)
Calyx = D or E (ribbon stitch)

### Leaves

Outer leaves = D or E (ribbon stitch, side ribbon stitch)
Inner leaves = D or E (looped ribbon stitch, ribbon stitch)

Stems = A (split back stitch)

Beads = G or H (beading)

**Wild Rose**

# TULIPS

## by Helen Eriksson

### This design uses
*Couching, Folded ribbon stitch,
Looped ribbon stitch Ribbon stitch,
Side ribbon stitch, Twisted straight stitch*

## Materials

### Ribbons
*YLI silk ribbon 7mm (⁵⁄₁₆") wide*
A = 20cm (8") no. 13 vy lt yellow
B = 40cm (16") no. 23 med lavender
C = 60cm (24") no. 32 pistachio green
D = 60cm (24") no. 33 dk
pistachio green
E = 20cm (8") no. 62 lt blue-green
F = 40cm (16") no. 129 lt burgundy
*Petals hand dyed silk ribbon 7mm
(⁵⁄₁₆") wide*
G = 70cm (28") nectarine

### Needle
No. 18 chenille needle

## Order of work
Use the photograph as a guide for
colour changes within the design.

### Apricot tulips
Using the lightest section of G, work
two ribbon stitches and one side ribbon
stitch for the inner petals of the left
hand tulip. Stitch each petal using the
same hole in the fabric at the base and
overlapping them slightly. Using the
darkest section of G, work a side ribbon
stitch on each side.

For the tulip at the top of the design,
work two overlapping ribbon stitches for
the inner petals. Add a side ribbon stitch
on each side and work a ribbon stitch
over the centre.

### Lavender tulips
For the tulip on the left, work a ribbon
stitch for the centre, two side ribbon
stitches for the inner petals and two side
ribbon stitches for the outer petals. Work
the remaining lavender tulip in the same
manner, omitting the centre petal.

### Burgundy tulips
Using G, work a ribbon stitch for the
centre of the left hand tulip. Work a
ribbon stitch over the top using F. Stitch
two ribbon stitches, using G, for the
inner petals and two side ribbon stitches
for the outer petals with F.

For the right hand tulip, thread the
needle with lengths of both the yellow
and burgundy ribbon. Work two inner
petals and one outer petal in ribbon
stitch and one outer petal in side ribbon
stitch, ensuring the burgundy ribbon is
on the top. When the stitches are worked
the yellow ribbon will peep out from the
top and sides of the burgundy ribbon.

### Stems and leaves
To work the stems for each tulip, bring
the ribbon to the front just under the
base of a tulip. Twist the ribbon until it
becomes thin. Take it to the back at the
base of the stem, forming a long
straight stitch.

Randomly work the leaves in ribbon
stitch, looped ribbon stitch and folded
ribbon stitch, using the various shades
of green. For the leaves that are worked
in folded ribbon stitch, work a small
couching stitch on the inside of the fold
to hold them in place.

### Apricot tulips

Inner petals = G (ribbon stitch)
Outer petals = G (side ribbon stitch, ribbon stitch) or none

### Lavender tulips

Centre = B (ribbon stitch) or none
Inner petals = B (side ribbon stitch)
Outer petals = B (side ribbon stitch)

### Burgundy tulip on left

Centre = G and F (ribbon stitch)
Inner petals = G (side ribbon stitch)
Outer petals = F (side ribbon stitch)

### Burgundy tulip on right

Inner petals = A and F together (ribbon stitch)
Outer petals = A and F together (ribbon stitch, side ribbon stitch)

### Stems and leaves

Stems = C or D (twisted straight stitch)
Leaves = C, D or E (ribbon stitch, looped ribbon stitch, folded ribbon stitch, couching)

# ROSE CORSAGE

## by Shirley Sinclair

### This design uses

*Folded and gathered rose, Folded ribbon rose, Wire-edged ribbon leaf*

### Ribbon embroidery endex

## Materials

### Ribbons

*Hand dyed rayon satin ribbon 50mm (2") wide*
A = 3m (3yd 10") rich cream/pink
*Wire-edged rayon ribbon 25mm (1") wide*
B = 35cm (14") olive green

### Needle

No. 8 crewel needle

### Supplies

Lace pins
Matching quilting thread
Gold stamens (approx 24 per bud)

## Order of work

### Rose, rosebuds and leaves

Make the rose, rosebuds and leaves following the step-by-step instructions.

## Assembling the corsage

After the rose, rosebuds and leaves have been completed, stitch the two buds to one side of the rose, tucking them slightly under the petals.

Stitch a leaf to the underside of the buds, so it is visible between them. Stitch the second leaf so it is between one bud and the rose.

### Embroidery key

Rose = A (folded and gathered rose)

Rosebuds = A (folded and gathered rosebud)

Leaves = B (wire-edged ribbon leaf)

# FOLDED AND GATHERED ROSE

**1 Centre.** Cut a 10cm (4") length of ribbon. Make a folded ribbon rose with four petals following the instructions on pages 14–15.

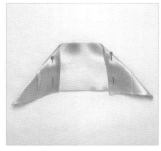

**2 Inner petals.** Cut a 15cm (6") length of ribbon. Fold each end to the back and pin.

3 Using the quilting thread, work a row of gathering stitches along the lower edge of the ribbon.

4 Pull up the gathers and secure. Make three more petals in the same manner.

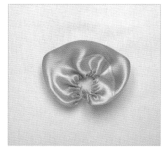

**5 Middle petals.** Cut four lengths of ribbon, each 18cm (7") long. Make four petals in the same manner as the inner petals.

**6 Outer petals.** Cut three lengths of ribbon, each 20cm (8") long and fashion three petals in the same manner as before.

**7 Attaching petals.** Wrap one inner petal around the centre of the rose, slightly over-lapping the ends. Secure at base with tiny back stitches.

8 Attach a second petal, taking it halfway around the base. Stitch in place as before.

9 Attach the third and fourth petals so the ends overlap.

10 Secure the four middle petals and the three outer petals in the same manner. **Completed rose.**

# WIRE-EDGED RIBBON LEAF

**1** Cut a 16cm (6 ¼") length of wire-edged ribbon. Fold in half across the width. Bring the folded end over diagonally.

**2** Fold the raw ends over. Work gathering stitches close to the folded end, along the edge and across the diagonal folded end.

**3** Pull up the gathers slightly and secure with several tiny back stitches.

**4** Open out the ribbon and shape into a leaf. **Completed ribbon leaf.**

# FOLDED & GATHERED ROSEBUDS

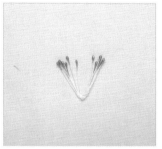

**1** Cut five lengths of ribbon 16cm (6 ¼") long and make five petals in the same manner as the inner petals of the rose.

**2** Place twelve stamens together and twist them slightly in the centre. Fold them in half.

**3** Lay the bunch of stamens on the lower edge of one petal at the centre. Stitch in place to secure.

**4** Wrap each end of the petal around the stamens. Secure at the base of the ribbon with 2–3 tiny back stitches. Do not pull the stitches too tight.

**5** Leave the thread dangling. Wrap a second petal around the first and secure at base in the same manner.

**6** Wrap a third petal loosely around the bud and secure as before.

**7** Work a second rosebud in the same manner, omitting the third petal. **Completed rosebuds.**

# CHERRY BLOSSOM

## by Angela Dower

### This design uses

*Back stitch, Couching, French knot,
Granitos, Long and short stitch,
Raised stem stitch Ribbon stitch,
Side ribbon stitch, Straight stitch,
Twisted detached chain,
Whipped back stitch*

### Ribbon Embroidery Index

Couching 11
Ribbon stitch 23
Side Ribbon stitch 26
Straight stitch 33
Twisted detached chain 13

## Materials

### Threads & ribbons

*DMC stranded cotton*
A = 3781 dk putty groundings
*Needle Necessities overdyed floss*
B = 147 copper pennies
*Rajmahal Art silk*
C = 93 chardonnay
D = 171 woodlands
*Au Ver à Soie, Soie d'Alger*
E = 2146 vy dk yellow green
*YLI silk floss*
F = 157 drab olive
G = 182 eggshell
*YLI silk ribbon 7mm (⁵⁄₁₆") wide*
H = 1m (39 ½") no. 6 baby pink
*Glen Lorin hand dyed silk ribbon 7mm
(⁵⁄₁₆") wide*
I = 1.2m (1yd 12") Annie's request
*Colour Streams hand dyed silk ribbon 4mm
(³⁄₁₆") wide*
J = 1m (39 ½") no. 26 Tuscan olive

### Needles

No. 9 straw (milliner's) needle
No. 18 chenille needle
No. 20 tapestry needle

## Order of work

Use the photograph as a guide for
thread colour changes within the design.

Use the straw needle for all thread
embroidery, the chenille needle for the
silk ribbons and the tapestry needle for
the whipping.

### Main stem

Outline the stem in back stitch then fill
with vertical long and short stitch for
padding. Using the darkest sections of B
first and then the lightest sections, work
2–3 rows of raised stem stitch. Work the
last few rows in A. Stitch a few vertical
straight stitches at the top of the stem.

### Flower stems and leaves

With the exception of one stem and leaf,
embroider the stems in whipped back
stitch, followed by the leaves. On the left
hand side, one stem is embroidered over
a leaf.

Start the leaves from the top of the
design and work towards the centre.

### Buds

Work a twisted detached chain for the
padding of the buds. Using the darkest
shade of I, work a straight stitch over the
twisted detached chain. Still using the
darkest shade of I, work two more
straight stitches each side of the
previous stitch, overlapping them at
the base.

Embroider the calyxes next, starting
with a tiny twisted detached chain
worked 2–3mm (⅛") away from the bud.
Work a ribbon stitch each side of the
bud, followed by a ribbon stitch
enclosing the tiny detached chain. Take
the ribbon through the base of the
centre petal.

Using a pair of tweezers, carefully
squeeze the ribbon stitch to elongate the
base of the bud. Couch in place at each
side of the ribbon.

## Flowers

Work a side view flower on each side of the stem and then a third one on the left hand side. Embroider a straight stitch for the centre, then a straight stitch each side that slightly overlaps the centre. Add three more straight stitches for the outer petals of two flowers and five for the remaining flower. Embroider the stamens using a long straight stitch with a granitos on the end, tucking the straight stitches just under the petals.

The calyxes are worked in a similar manner to those on the buds, except the ribbon stitches are folded back and the lower section is couched in place (*diag 1*).

The facing flower is worked with four ribbon stitch petals and a straight stitch petal over the leaves. Stitch the stamens over the petals, placing a French knot at the end of each one.

Place the side view open flower just to the right of the facing flower. Work a straight stitch in the centre, then a ribbon stitch each side just overlapping the centre at the base. Stitch the two back petals in ribbon stitch. The calyx is worked with a tiny twisted detached chain covered with a straight stitch. Embroider a green straight stitch with a French knot for the central stamen. All the remaining stamens are worked in the same manner as the side view flowers except where the ends are on the ribbon. Work these with a French knot.

## Embroidery key

*All thread embroidery is worked with one strand.*

### Stems

Main stem padding = A (back stitch, long and short stitch)
Main stem = A and B (raised stem stitch, straight stitch)
Flower stems = E (whipped back stitch)

### Leaves = J (ribbon stitch, side ribbon stitch)

### Buds

Petals = H (twisted detached chain), I (straight stitch)
Calyx = J (twisted detached chain, ribbon stitch, straight stitch), F (couching)

### Side view flowers

Petals = H and I (straight stitch)
Calyx = J (twisted detached chain, straight stitch, ribbon stitch), F (couching)
Stamens = C, D and F (straight stitch, granitos)

### Facing flower

Petals = I (ribbon stitch, straight stitch)
Central stamen = E (straight stitch, French knot, 1 wrap)
Remaining stamens = G (straight stitch), C or D (French knot, 1 wrap)

### Side view open flower

Petals = H and I (straight stitch, ribbon stitch)
Calyx = J (twisted detached chain, straight stitch)
Central stamen = E (straight stitch, French knot, 1 wrap)
Remaining stamens = G (straight stitch), C or D (granitos, French knot, 1 wrap)

*The Peony*

*Diag 1*

# BRIAR ROSE

by Carolyn Pearce

## This design uses

*Beading, Colonial knot, Couching,
Fly stitch, French knot, Long and short stitch,
Pistil stitch, Ribbon stitch, Side ribbon stitch,
Smocker's knot, Split stitch, Straight stitch,
Twisted detached chain, Whipped stem stitch*

### Ribbon embroidery index

Briar rose 60
Ribbon rosebud 24
Ribbon stitch 23
Side ribbon stitch 26
Twisted detached chain 13

## Materials

### Threads, ribbons & beads

Grey machine sewing thread
Clear nylon thread
*Au Ver à Soie, Soie d'Alger*
A = 2133 med olive green
B = 2636 vy dk copper
C = 2926 vy dk brick red
D = 3735 dk slate
E = 3744 taupe
F = 3745 dk taupe
G = 4233 med wheat gold
H = F1 ecru
I = F19 chicken soup
*YLI silk floss*
J = 000 bright white
*Gumnut Yarns 'Opals' wool/silk thread*
K = dark topaz
*Colour Streams 'Ophir' fine silk thread*
L = 26 Tuscan olive
*Au Ver à Soie antique metallic thread*
M = 210 black copper
N = 520 red copper
*YLI silk ribbon 4mm (³⁄₁₆") wide*
O = 40cm (16") no. 107 lt terracotta
*YLI hand dyed silk ribbon 4mm (³⁄₁₆") wide*
P = 70cm (27 ½") no. 520 eucalyptus
*Petals hand dyed silk ribbon 4mm (³⁄₁₆") wide*
Q = 30cm (12") copper rose
*Tooray Sillook polyester ribbon 4mm (³⁄₁₆") wide*
R = 1m (39 ½") no. 425B daphne pink
*Vintage ribbons hand dyed silk ribbon 7mm (⁵⁄₁₆") wide*
S = 80cm (31 ½") soft terracotta
*Mill Hill petite glass beads*
T = 42011 Victorian gold

### Needles

No. 5 crewel needle
No. 8 crewel needle
No. 10 crewel needle
No. 12 crewel needle
No. 18 chenille needle
No. 22 chenille needle

### Supplies

Small brass butterfly
Small amount of grey felt
Small amount of paper backed fusible webbing (eg *Vliesofix*)

## Order of work

Use the no. 18 chenille needle for the 7mm (⁵⁄₁₆") ribbon and the no. 22 chenille needle for the 4mm (³⁄₁₆") ribbons. Use the no. 5 crewel needle when working with five strands of silk thread and the no. 8 crewel needle when working with three strands of silk thread, 'Opals' and 'Ophir' threads. The nos. 10 and 12 crewel needles are used for all other embroidery and the beading.

### Briar roses

Work the two briar roses first. Embroider the stem with one row of stem stitch. Work a second row from the base to half way up the side of the first row. Whip the two rows together and continue along the single row.

### Rosebuds

Embroider a pair of rosebuds on each side of the design. Work the stems in stem stitch followed by the silk ribbon leaves. Each leaf is a twisted detached chain with a straight stitch at the tip and a smocker's knot at the base.

### Fly stitch leaves and stems

Work the stems in whipped stem stitch, then stitch the two groups of five leaves in fly stitch. Work a smocker's knot at the base of each leaf.

### Rosehips

For the lower pair of rosehips, work the stem in two rows of stem stitch, worked side by side, up to where the stems divide. Continue the stems with single rows of stem stitch. Whip the two lower rows together then whip the single rows. Work the stems of the upper pair with whipped stem stitch.

Each rosehip is padded with three layers of felt, each one slightly larger than the previous one. Trace the padding templates onto the fusible webbing. Fuse the webbing to the felt then cut out each shape. Attach the felt pieces, one at a time, with tiny stitches, starting with the smallest and ending with the largest.

Beginning at the base, completely cover the padding with long and short stitch. Change thread colour and work long and short stitch over the top left hand corner of each rosehip. Add the highlights with five to ten straight stitches. At the tip of each rosehip, work tiny pistil stitches of varying lengths for the stamens.

### Queen Anne's lace

Work the main stems and flower stems in split stitch. Add a pistil stitch to the end of each flower stem. Attach a tiny gold bead just above the end of each pistil stitch. Embroider cream French knots and colonial knots around the tops of the flower stems.

### Violets

Embroider each violet with five ribbon stitch petals, working them in the order shown (*diag 1*).

Stitch three or four straight stitches over the three lower petals for highlights. Work a colonial knot for each centre. Embroider a pair of wispy fly stitches for the leaves of each violet.

*Diag 1*

### Butterfly

Using the clear nylon thread, attach the small brass butterfly just above the upper right rosebud.

## Embroidery key

*All thread embroidery is worked with one strand unless otherwise specified.*

### Briar roses

Petals = S (side ribbon stitch)
Centre = 1 strand of F blended with 2 strands each of G and M (5 strands, colonial knot)
Highlights = N (straight stitch)
Stem = D (2 strands, whipped stem stitch)

### Rosebuds

Centre = O (twisted detached chain)
Petals = Q (ribbon stitch)
Tip = E (straight stitch)
Calyx = P (ribbon stitch), E (fly stitch, smocker's knot, straight stitch)
Stems = K and D (whipped stem stitch)
Leaves = P (twisted detached chain), E (straight stitch, smocker's knot)

### Fly stitch leaves and stems

Leaves = L (fly stitch, smocker's knot)
Stems = K and D (whipped stem stitch)

### Rosehips

Hips = B and C (long and short stitch)
Highlights = N (straight stitch)
Stamens = M (pistil stitch)
Stems = F (2 strands, split stitch)

### Queen Anne's lace

Main stems = A (split stitch)
Flower stems = A (split stitch, pistil stitch)
Flowers = H or I (colonial knot, French knot, 1 wrap), H (2 strands, colonial knot, French knot, 1 wrap), T (beading)

### Violets

Petals = R (ribbon stitch)
Petal highlights = J (straight stitch)
Centre = 1 strand of B blended with 2 strands of G (colonial knot)
Leaves = D (fly stitch)

*Butterfly* = brass butterfly, clear nylon thread (couching)

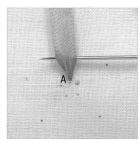

**1 Petals.** Bring the ribbon to the front at A. Smooth and spread the ribbon.

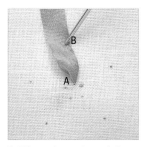

**2** Place the point of the needle just in from the edge of the ribbon at B.

**3** Hold the ribbon in place to keep it flat and untwisted (thumb not shown). Begin to pull the ribbon through.

**4** Pull until the ribbon folds back on itself and the upper edge curls. Pulling too far will result in a thin stitch.

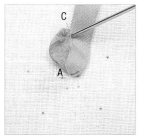

**5** Bring the ribbon to the front just to the right of A. Lay ribbon beside first stitch. Place the needle on the opposite side of ribbon at C.

**6** Complete the stitch as before.

**7** Work two more petals in the same manner, positioning them as shown.

**8** Work a petal in the two upper spaces.

**9 Centre and highlights.** Stitch five colonial knots in the centre and 2–3 straight stitches on each petal. **Completed briar rose.**

# SMALL DAFFODILS

## by Helen Eriksson

### This design uses

*Folded ribbon stitch, Grab stitch,
Looped ribbon stitch Ribbon stitch,
Stem stitch, Straight stitch*

### Ribbon embroidery index

Daffodil 40
Folded ribbon stitch 24
Looped ribbon stitch 25
Ribbon stitch 23

### Materials

#### Thread & ribbons

*Anchor stranded cotton*
A = 268 vy dk avocado green
*YLI silk ribbon 4mm (³⁄₁₆") wide*
B = 40cm (16") no. 3 vy lt yellow
C = 70cm (28") no. 14 lt yellow
D = 1m (39 ½") no. 20 forest green
E = 1m (39 ½") no. 54 old gold

#### Needles

No. 8 crewel needle
No. 20 chenille needle

### Order of work

Use the chenille needle for the ribbon
embroidery and the crewel needle for
the thread embroidery.

### Daffodils

Work each flower head following the
step-by-step instructions. Work the
frilled edge of the trumpet with a single
row of looped ribbon stitches rather
than an oval.

### Buds

Embroider the buds with a central
ribbon stitch in the gold ribbon. Using
the pale lemon ribbon, work a longer
ribbon stitch on each side of the centre
to partially cover it.

### Stems

Work the flower stems in stem stitch.
Start the bud stems at the base of each
bud with a grab stitch. Change to stem
stitch to complete the stem.

### Leaves

Beginning at the base, embroider the
leaves in folded ribbon stitch. Add short
straight stitches over the lower ends of
some of the leaves for leaf veins.

### Embroidery key

*All thread embroidery is worked with
one strand.*

#### Flowers

Petals = B and C (ribbon stitch)
Trumpet = E (ribbon stitch)
Trumpet frill = E (looped
ribbon stitch)
Stem = A (stem stitch)

#### Buds

Centre = E (ribbon stitch)
Petals = C (ribbon stitch)
Stems = A (grab stitch, stem stitch)

*Leaves* = D (folded ribbon stitch), A
(straight stitch)

# CARNATIONS

by Helen Eriksson

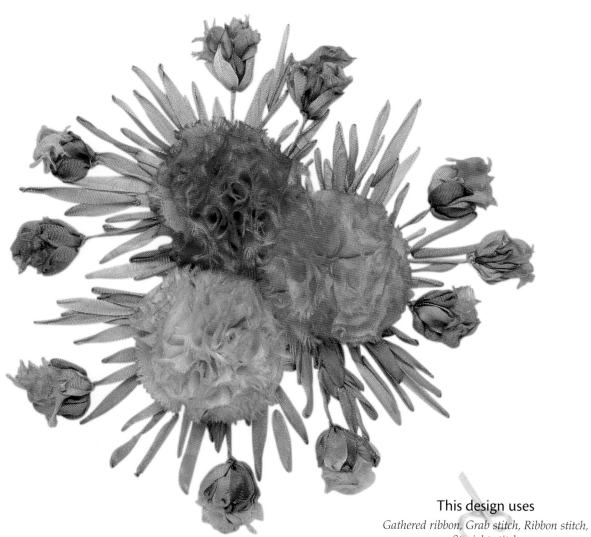

**This design uses**
*Gathered ribbon, Grab stitch, Ribbon stitch,*
*Straight stitch*

### Ribbon embroidery index

## Materials

### Threads & ribbons

Machine sewing threads to match
the ribbons
*Hanah hand dyed bias cut silk ribbon
15mm (⅝") wide*
A = 1.5m (1yd 23") cherry blossom
B = 1.5m (1yd 23") china doll
C = 1.5m (1yd 23") lingerie
*Kacoonda hand dyed silk ribbon 4mm
(3⁄16") wide*
D = 4m (4yd 14") no. 104 sage green
*Kacoonda hand dyed silk ribbon 7mm
(5⁄16") wide*
E = 1.6m (1yd 27") no. 104 sage green

### Needles

No. 8 sharp needle
No. 16 chenille needle
No. 18 chenille needle

## Order of work

Refer to the photograph as a guide for
colour placement.

Use the no. 18 chenille needle for the
7mm (5⁄16") ribbon and the no. 16
chenille needle for the 4mm (3⁄16")
ribbon. Use the sharp needle for the
sewing thread.

### Fraying the pink ribbons

Hold a length of the pink ribbon
between your thumbs and forefingers.
While stretching the ribbon, run one
edge between your thumb and
forefinger to fray it. Continue fraying
along the entire length of the ribbon on
one edge only. You may need to repeat
the process several times. Prepare the
remaining two pink ribbons in the same
manner. Dyes often have different
effects on ribbon and sometimes an
edge will not fray easily. If this happens,
change to the other edge of the ribbon
and try again.

### Flowers

Cut a 70cm (28") length of ribbon from
each of the three pink ribbons. The
remaining lengths of ribbon are for the
buds. Form the three carnations and
stitch them to the centre of the design.

### Buds

Using the remaining frayed pink
ribbons, work the petals of each bud
with two loose ribbon stitches that
slightly overlap each other. Ensure the
frayed edge is on the left hand side for
one stitch and on the right hand side for
the other stitch. Beginning at the base
and ending halfway up the bud, add the
calyx with four to six loose
ribbon stitches.

### Stems and leaves

Starting at the base of each bud, begin
to work a grab stitch. Before anchoring
the stitch, twist the ribbon. Anchor the
stitch beneath the petals of the
carnations. Work the leaves in straight
and ribbon stitches, randomly placing
them around the carnations.

### Embroidery key

*Flowers* = A, B and C (gathered ribbon)

*Buds*
Petals = A, B and C (ribbon stitch)
Calyx = E (ribbon stitch)

*Stems* = D (grab stitch)

*Leaves* = D (ribbon stitch, straight stitch)

*Safe Journey*

# CARNATION

1 Hold ribbon horizontally with the frayed edge at the top. Fold over the right hand end of the ribbon diagonally.

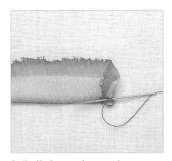

2 Roll the end over three times and secure at the lower edge with 2–3 tiny stitches through the roll.

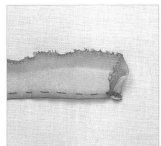

3 Beginning at the folded end, work running stitches approx 4mm (³⁄₁₆") long, close to the lower edge for approx 12cm (4 ¾").

4 Pull up the thread to gather the ribbon tightly. Secure at the base with 2–3 tiny stitches through all layers.

5 Work running stitches in the same manner along the next 12cm (4 ¾") of ribbon.

6 Pull up gathers and hold them firmly. With lower edge of ribbon even, roll the new gathered section anticlockwise onto the centre roll.

7 Secure through all layers at the base as before. Continue in the same manner until approx 12cm (4 ¾") from the end of the ribbon.

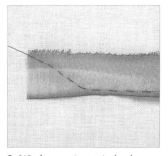

8 Work running stitch along edge until 2cm (¾") from the end. Continue diagonally across ribbon, finishing 4mm (³⁄₁₆") from end on top edge.

9 Trim away the excess ribbon leaving 3mm (⅛") of ribbon beyond the running stitches.

10 Pull up the gathers. Secure as before. Leave the thread dangling.

11 Take thread to back of fabric at position for flower centre. Spread petals. Bring thread to front through the flower. Donot catch any petals.

12 Continue working several stab stitches through the flower.
**Completed carnation.**

# DUTCH HYACINTHS

## by Helen Eriksson

## Order of work

Use the no. 22 chenille needle for the 4mm (³⁄₁₆") ribbons and the no. 20 chenille needle for the 7mm (⁵⁄₁₆") ribbons.

### Flowers

Begin with the hyacinth on the right hand side using C. Stitch five or six very tiny looped ribbon stitches for the first floret within the flower head. To keep the stitches plump, hold the ribbon over a large needle while completing the stitch. Keeping the ribbon stitches close together, work enough florets to fill the rectangular shape. Stitch the middle hyacinth with E and the remaining hyacinth with D.

### Stems

Bring the needle to the front at the bottom of each flower head, twist the ribbon several times and take to the back at the base of the design.

### Leaves

Using the two shades of green, add the leaves with a mixture of ribbon stitches and folded ribbon stitches. Couch the leaves at any folds.

## This design uses

*Couching, Folded ribbon stitch, Looped ribbon stitch, Ribbon stitch, Twisted straight stitch*

### Ribbon embroidery index

Couching 11
Folded ribbon stitch 24
Looped ribbon stitch 25
Ribbon stitch 23
Twisted straight stitch 34

## Materials

### Ribbons

*YLI silk ribbon 7mm (⁵⁄₁₆") wide*
A = 50cm (20") no. 32 med pistachio
B = 50cm (20") no. 33 dk pistachio
*Kacoonda hand dyed silk ribbon 4mm (³⁄₁₆") wide*
C = 1m (39 ½") no. 3 lt antique blue-violet
D = 1m (39 ½") no. 3B dk blue-violet
*Colour Streams hand dyed silk ribbon 4mm (³⁄₁₆") wide*
E = 1m (39 ½") no. 24 plum

### Needles

No. 20 chenille needle
No. 22 chenille needle

## Embroidery key

*Flowers* = C, D or E (looped ribbon stitch)

*Stems* = B (twisted straight stitch)

*Leaves* = A or B (ribbon stitch, folded ribbon stitch, couching)

*Revival*

# RAMBLING ROSES

## by Carolyn Pearce

## This design uses

*Cabbage rose, Colonial knot,
Detached chain, Fly stitch, Loop stitch,
Ribbon stitch, Running stitch – colonial
knot combination, Smocker's knot,
Spider web rose, Straight stitch,
Twirled ribbon rose, Twisted detached chain,
Whipped stem stitch*

### Ribbon embroidery index

Cabbage rose petal 68
Colonial knot 9
Loop stitch 19
Loop stitch flower 21
Ribbon rosebud 24
Ribbon stitch 23
Running stitch – colonial knot
combination 28
Spider web rose 30
Twirled ribbon rose 36
Twisted detached chain 13

## Materials

### Threads & ribbons

Machine sewing thread to match
silk ribbons
*DMC stranded cotton*
A = 640 vy dk beige-grey
B = 642 dk beige-grey
*Kacoonda 2 ply silk*
C = 305 dk dusky blue
*Kacoonda fine silk*
D = 104 sage green
E = 106 antique green
*Au Papillon metallic thread*
F = antique gold
*YLI silk floss*
G = 181 gold-beige
*YLI metallic yarn*
H = 403 jade green
*Colour Streams 'Ophir' fine silk*
I = 26 Tuscan olive
*Kacoonda hand dyed silk ribbon 13mm
(½") wide*
J = 25cm (10") no. 6C autumn rose
K = 25cm (10") no. 101 sunset rose
L = 15cm (6") no. 310 dusky rose pink
*YLI silk ribbon 4mm (³⁄₁₆") wide*
M = 50cm (20") no. 158 dusky pink
*YLI silk ribbon 7mm (⁵⁄₁₆") wide*

N = 15cm (6") no. 159 vy dk dusky pink
*YLI silk ribbon 13mm (½") wide*
O = 15cm (6") no. 163 med dusky pink
*Colour Streams hand dyed silk ribbon 4mm
(³⁄₁₆")*
P = 1m (39 ½") no. 23 rose blush
*Colour Streams hand dyed silk ribbon 7mm
(⁵⁄₁₆")*
Q = 30cm (12") no. 23 rose blush
*Vintage ribbons silk ribbon 4mm (³⁄₁₆") wide*
R = 1m (39 ½") pine needles
*The Thread Gatherer Silken Ribbons silk
ribbon 4mm (³⁄₁₆") wide*
S = 50cm (20") heirloom blue
*Tooray Sillook polyester ribbon 4mm
(³⁄₁₆") wide*
T = 30cm (12") no. 835 old gold

### Needles

No. 5 crewel needle
No. 8 crewel needle
No. 10 crewel needle
No. 10 straw (milliner's) needle
No. 12 sharp needle
No. 18 chenille needle
No. 22 chenille needle

### Supplies

Lace pins

## Order of work

*Refer to the needle chart on the following page.*

### Cabbage rose

Cut the following ribbons into 25mm (1") lengths. Cut four pieces from J, five pieces from K, three pieces using the deepest tones of L and two pieces from O. Form each piece into a gathered petal.

Using N, work a very loose colonial knot for the centre. Arrange the petals around the centre and stitch in place using matching machine sewing thread.

### Medium roses

Stitch three twirled ribbon roses next to the cabbage rose. Embroider a spider web rose alongside the previous roses.

### Small roses

Work three running stitch – colonial knot combination roses in a tight cluster next to the spider web rose.

### Rosebuds

Stitch the six rosebuds following the step-by-step instructions. Add an extra fly stitch and straight stitch to each one, using the gold metallic thread.

### Stems and leaves

Embroider the stems in whipped stem stitch, using the dark beige-grey thread for the stem stitch and the antique gold for the whipping. Work the fly stitch leaves next. Three rosebud leaves have straight stitch highlights worked over the fly stitches. Finish each leaf with a smocker's knot at the base.

Work two pairs of twisted detached chain leaves, in ribbon, near the cluster of smaller roses. Add a straight stitch using thread over the anchoring stitch.

### Forget-me-nots

Embroider three large forget-me-nots using five loop stitches for the petals of each one. Add a single colonial knot for the centre.

Tiny forget-me-nots are scattered among the roses and leaves. Work five colonial knots for the petals of each flower and a single colonial knot for each centre. Stitch pairs of detached chain leaves close to some of the forget-me-nots.

## Embroidery key

*All thread embroidery is worked with one strand unless otherwise specified.*

### Cabbage rose

Centre = N (colonial knot)
First round of petals = L (3 cabbage rose petals)
Second round of petals = K (4 cabbage rose petals)
Third round of petals = K (1 cabbage rose petal), I (1 cabbage rose petal), O (2 cabbage rose petals)
Fourth round of petals = J (3 cabbage rose petals)

*Medium roses* = Q (twirled ribbon rose), P (spider web rose)

*Small roses* = P (running stitch – colonial knot combination)

### Rosebuds

Centre = M (twisted detached chain)
Petals = P (ribbon stitch)
Tip = A (straight stitch)
Calyx = R (ribbon stitch), A and F (fly stitch, straight stitch)

### Stems and leaves

Stems = A and F (whipped stem stitch)
Cabbage rose leaves = E or I (fly stitch, smocker's knot)

Rosebud leaves = D and H (fly stitch, straight stitch, smocker's knot), H (fly stitch, smocker's knot)
Ribbon leaves = R (twisted detached chain), A (straight stitch)

### Large forget-me-nots

Petals = S (loop stitch)
Centre = T (colonial knot)

### Tiny forget-me-nots

Petals = C (colonial knot)
Centre = G (colonial knot)
Leaves = B (detached chain) or none

*Spellbound*

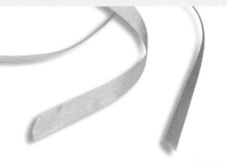

| No. 5 crewel | No. 8 crewel | No. 10 crewel | No. 10 straw | No. 12 sharp | No. 18 chenille | No. 22 chenille |
|---|---|---|---|---|---|---|
| Colour Streams 'Ophir' | Antique gold thread on the rosebuds & stems | DMC stranded cotton | YLI metallic yarn | Spokes of the spider web rose | All 7mm (5/16") ribbons | All 4mm (3/16") ribbons |
| Kacoonda 2 ply silk | Kacoonda fine silk | | Curling petals for cabbage rose | Matching machine sewing thread | | |
| | YLI silk floss | | | | | |

# CABBAGE ROSE PETAL

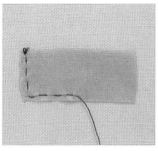

**1** Cut a 26mm (1") length of ribbon. Using a knotted thread, work tiny running stitches along left end and approx halfway along lower edge. Leave thread dangling.

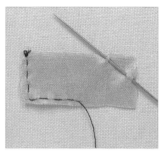

**2** Pin the straw needle diagonally across the top right corner.

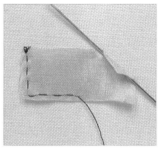

**3** Fold the corner of the ribbon over the needle.

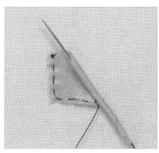

**4** Roll the ribbon tightly until the needle lines up with both ends of the running stitch.

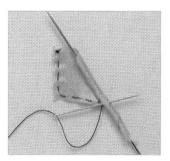

**5** Pick up the dangling thread. Take a stitch through the roll.

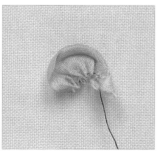

**6** Remove the straw needle. Pull up the running stitches so the petal cups slightly.

**7** Secure the thread with two back stitches and cut off the excess thread.

**8** Carefully trim the tail of ribbon near the back stitches and trim any whiskers of ribbon or thread. **Completed cabbage rose petal.**

# PANSIES

## by Gabrielle Francis

### This design uses

*Bullion loop, Detached chain, French knot, Ribbon stitch, Satin stitch, Stem stitch, Straight stitch*

**Ribbon embroidery index**

Ribbon stitch 23

## Materials

### Threads & ribbons

*Anchor stranded cotton*
A = 9 coral
B = 873 vy dk antique violet
C = 924 vy dk olive
*YLI silk ribbon 4mm (³⁄₁₆") wide*
D = 50cm (20") no. 15 bright yellow
E = 50cm (20") no. 20 forest green
F = 30cm (12") no. 101 blue-violet
G = 40cm (16") no. 117 hyacinth

### Needles

No. 9 straw (milliner's) needle
No. 9 crewel needle
No. 22 chenille needle

## Order of work

Use the chenille needle for the ribbons, the straw needle for the bullion loops and the crewel needle for all other thread embroidery.

### Flowers

Embroider the pansy flowers first, working the upper petals, then the lower and side petals. Stitch six to eight straight stitches over the side and lower petals, ensuring they radiate from the centre of the flower.

Add a French knot for the centre of the upper pansy and a tiny bullion loop for the centres of the two lower pansies.

### Stems, buds and leaves

Embroider the stems for the pansies and buds in stem stitch, tucking some of the stitches just under the petals of the pansies.

Work the buds in ribbon stitch. For the calyxes, stitch one to three small straight stitches over the base of the petals. Work tiny satin stitches across the base of the bud on the left and the two lower buds on the right. For the two upper buds on the right, work a pair of straight stitches along each petal and two or three detached chains for the calyx.

Stitch the leaves at the lower ends of the stems in ribbon stitch.

## Embroidery key

*All thread embroidery is worked with one strand.*

### Flowers

Upper petals = G (ribbon stitch)
Middle petals = F (ribbon stitch)
Lower petals = D (ribbon stitch)
Petal markings = B (straight stitch)
Centre = A (French knot, 1 wrap or bullion loop, 6–8 wraps)

### Buds

Petals = G (ribbon stitch)
Calyx = C (straight stitch, satin stitch or straight stitch, detached chain)

### Stems and leaves

Stems = C (stem stitch)
Leaves = E (ribbon stitch)

# LILY OF THE VALLEY

## by Angela Dower

### This design uses

*Back stitch, Couching, Long and short stitch, Raised stem stitch, Ribbon stitch, Side ribbon stitch, Stem stitch, Straight stitch, Twisted detached chain, Whipped back stitch*

## Materials

### Threads & ribbons

*DMC stranded cotton*
A = 3013 lt khaki green
*Madeira stranded cotton*
B = 1408 avocado green
C = 1602 dk khaki green
*YLI silk floss*
D = 0 natural white
*YLI silk ribbon 4mm (³⁄₁₆") wide*
E = 2m (2yd 7") no. 1 antique white
F = 2m (2yd 7") no. 156 cream
*YLI silk ribbon 7mm (⁵⁄₁₆") wide*
G = 1.5m (1yd 23") no. 156 cream
*Glen Lorin hand dyed silk ribbon 2mm (¹⁄₈") wide*
H = 60cm (24") burnt sands

### Needles

No. 9 crewel needle
No. 18 chenille needle
No. 22 chenille needle
No. 20 tapestry needle
No. 26 tapestry needle

### Supplies

Lace pins

## Order of work

Use the no. 22 chenille needle for the 2mm (¹⁄₈") ribbon and the no.18 chenille needle for the 4mm (³⁄₁₆") and 7mm (⁵⁄₁₆") ribbons. The no. 20 tapestry needle is used for the whipping and the no. 26 tapestry needle for working the raised stem stitch. Work all other thread embroidery with the crewel needle.

## Main stems

The stems are worked in three sections. Outline the stem in back stitch and fill the lower section with vertical long and short stitches for padding. Add evenly spaced horizontal straight stitches along this section of the stem to form the framework for the raised stem stitch. Work raised stem stitch over the padding using the darker thread for the outer edges and the lighter threads for the central area.

Stitch the middle section with two rows of stem stitch. Embroider the top section in two rows of back stitch. Keep the stitch length even. Working towards the tip, whip the back stitches together. Turn the work upside down and whip over the back stitches a second time.

## Small flower stems

Work the small flower stems in the same manner as the top section of the main stems, whipping the back stitch once. Add a ribbon stitch for the hoods of most of the flowers.

## Flowers

Using the cream ribbon, work a twisted detached chain for the padding of each flower. Use the 4mm (³⁄₁₆") ribbon for padding the flowers which are worked over the main stems and the 7mm (⁵⁄₁₆") ribbon for the remaining flowers. Work the side petals, using the cream ribbon for the left hand side and the white ribbon for the right hand side. For each one, coax the ribbon into a slightly curled position at the tip and hold in place with a lace pin. Complete the stitch and couch the ribbon in place.

Work two ribbon stitch petals over the top of the padding. Partially cover the side petals.

## Buds

Embroider a twisted detached chain for the padding of each bud using the 7mm (⁵⁄₁₆") ribbon for the large bud and the 4mm (³⁄₁₆") ribbon for the smaller bud. Using the narrow ribbon, work a straight stitch on each side of the padding and a straight stitch over the top.

### Embroidery key

*All thread embroidery is worked with one strand unless otherwise specified.*

#### Main stems

Lower section = C (back stitch, long and short stitch), A, B and C (raised stem stitch)
Middle section = B and C (1 strand of each, stem stitch), B (2 strands, stem stitch)
Top section = B (whipped back stitch)

#### Flower stems

Stems = B (whipped back stitch)
Hoods = H (side ribbon stitch) or none

#### Flowers

Padding = F or G (twisted detached chain)
Side petals = E and F (side ribbon stitch), D (couching)
Outer petals = E and F (ribbon stitch)

#### Buds

Padding = F or G (twisted detached chain)
Side petals = E and F (straight stitch)
Outer petals = E (straight stitch)

# IRISES

## by Helen Eriksson

### This design uses

*Couching, Detached chain, Folded ribbon stitch, Grab stitch, Looped ribbon stitch, Ribbon stitch, Side ribbon stitch, Straight stitch, Twisted straight stitch*

## Materials

### Ribbons

*Petals hand dyed silk ribbon 7mm (⁵⁄₁₆") wide*
A = 70cm (28") black cherries
*YLI silk ribbon 7mm (⁵⁄₁₆") wide*
B = 50cm (20") no. 20 forest green
C = 50cm (20") no. 72 dk olive green
*YLI silk ribbon 4mm (³⁄₁₆") wide*
D = 30cm (12") no. 22 lt lavender
E = 30cm (12") no. 23 lavender
F = 20cm (8") no. 54 old gold
G = 60cm (24") no. 85 purple
H = 60cm (24") no. 171 avocado green

### Needles

No. 18 chenille needle
No. 20 chenille needle

## Order of work

Use the photograph as a guide for colour changes within the design.

The no. 18 chenille needle is used for the 7mm (⁵⁄₁₆") ribbons and the no. 20 chenille needle is used for the 4mm (³⁄₁₆") ribbons.

## Flowers

Embroider the large flower on the lower right hand side first. Stitch the three upper petals in closely worked ribbon stitch. For the lower petals, work a large open detached chain with two loosely worked side ribbon stitches over the top. Embroider a looped ribbon stitch at each side of the top petals, tucking the ends underneath. Work a small gold ribbon stitch for the centre.

Work the central iris next with two ribbon stitches for the upper petals and a detached chain with a ribbon stitch over the top for the lower petals. Stitch the two side petals and the centre in the same manner as before.

For the four small irises, work the upper petals with three ribbon stitches. The lower petals, side petals and centres are worked in the same manner as the central iris, with the exception of the top one. This iris has two ribbon stitches on each side for the side petals.

## Buds

Stitch the petals for the buds using one to three ribbon stitches.

### Calyxes, stems and leaves

To work the stems for each iris, bring the ribbon to the front just under the base of a flower. Twist the ribbon until it becomes thin. Take it to the back at the base of the stem, forming a long straight stitch.

Work the calyx and stem of the bud at the top with two straight stitches and a grab stitch. Stitch the calyxes for the remaining buds with a straight stitch on each side of the petals. Work the stems in the same manner as the flower stems.

Randomly work the leaves in ribbon stitch and looped ribbon stitch. For the leaves that are worked in folded ribbon stitch, work a small couching stitch on the inside of the fold of each bent leaf.

## Embroidery key

### Large flower

Upper petals = A (ribbon stitch)
Lower petals = A (detached chain, side ribbon stitch)
Side petals = A (looped ribbon stitch)
Centre = F (ribbon stitch)

### Small flowers

Upper petals = D, E or G (ribbon stitch)
Lower petals = D, E or G (detached chain, ribbon stitch)
Side petals = D, E or G (looped ribbon stitch)
Centre = F (ribbon stitch)

### Stems and leaves

Flower stems = B or C (twisted straight stitch)
Bud stems = B or H (twisted straight stitch)
Leaves = B, C or H (ribbon stitch, folded ribbon stitch, looped ribbon stitch, couching)

### Buds

Petals = A, E or G (ribbon stitch)
Calyxes = H (straight stitch, grab stitch)

*Silken Ribbons*

# JONQUILS

## by Helen Eriksson

### This design uses

*Couching, Fly stitch, Folded ribbon stitch, French knot, Grab stitch, Ribbon stitch, Straight stitch, Twisted straight stitch*

### Materials

*Ribbons*

*YLI silk ribbon 2mm (⅛") wide*
A = 80cm (31 ½") no. 20 forest green
*YLI silk ribbon 4mm (³⁄₁₆") wide*
B = 60cm (24") no. 15 bright yellow
C = 1m (39 ½") no. 33 dk pistachio green
D = 1m (39 ½") no. 54 old gold
E = 70cm (28") no. 106 apricot

*Needles*

No. 20 chenille needle
No. 22 chenille needle

### Order of work

Use the photograph as a guide for colour changes within the design.

The no. 20 chenille needle is used for the 4mm (³⁄₁₆") ribbons and the no. 22 chenille needle is used for the 2mm (⅛") ribbon.

Work the three main stems first, using a tightly twisted straight stitch.

Embroider the petals for the facing flowers with five very loose ribbon stitches and a single ribbon stitch for each bud. Stitch a French knot in the centre of each facing flower.

Using the green ribbons, work tiny straight stitches in between the flowers and buds. Stitch a fly stitch around some of the buds and a grab stitch or straight stitches around the remaining buds.

Embroider the leaves in straight stitch and folded ribbon stitch. Couch the folds with tiny straight stitches. To make the leaves with a hooked end, work a straight stitch, then work a shorter straight stitch, angling it from the top down and twisting it to make it thinner.

### Embroidery key

*Flowers*

Petals = B or D (ribbon stitch)
Centre = E (French knot, 2–3 wraps)

*Buds*

Petals = B or D (ribbon stitch)
Calyx = A or C (straight stitch, fly stitch, grab stitch)

*Stems and leaves*

Stems = A or C (twisted straight stitch)
Leaves = A or C (straight stitch, folded ribbon stitch, twisted straight stitch, couching)

# SPRING GARDEN

## by Jessica Wooderson

### This design uses

*Beading, Colonial knot, Fly stitch,
Folded ribbon rose, Gathering, Loop stitch
Ribbon stitch, Straight stitch*

### Ribbon embroidery index

Colonial knot 9
Folded ribbon rose 14
Gathered ribbon leaf 75
Loop stitch 19
Pansy 76
Ribbon stitch 23
Straight stitch 33

## Materials

### Threads, ribbons & beads

Matching machine sewing thread
*DMC stranded cotton*
A = 3012 med khaki green
*Kacoonda hand dyed silk ribbon 4mm
(³⁄₁₆") wide*
B = 1m (39 ½") no. 306 khaki green
*Kacoonda hand dyed silk ribbon 7mm
(⁵⁄₁₆") wide*
C = 1m (39 ½") no. 5 lt pansy
D = 1.5m (1yd 23") no. 5A pansy
E = 1.5m (1yd 23") no. 301 lt rose
F = 1m (39 ½") no. 103 golden sunset
G = 1m (39 ½") no. 104 sage green
*Mill Hill petite glass beads*
H = 42018 crystal pink
I = 42030 Victorian copper

### Needles

No. 9 crewel needle
No. 18 chenille needle
No. 22 chenille needle
Beading needle

### Supplies

White beading thread (eg *Nymo*)

## Order of work

Use the photograph as a guide for
colour changes within the design.

Use the no. 18 chenille needle for the
7mm (⁵⁄₁₆") ribbon and the no. 22
chenille needle for the 4mm (³⁄₁₆")
ribbon. The beading needle is used for
attaching the beads and the crewel
needle for all thread embroidery.

### Large central roses

Embroider the three loop stitch roses in
the centre of the design. Each rose has
five petals in varying shades of the light
pansy, light rose and golden sunset silk
ribbons. Attach five copper beads in the
centre of each rose.

Using ribbon stitch, work the leaves
next, tucking them under the loops of
the rose petals.

### Pansies

Make nine gathered ribbon leaves and
secure to the fabric with tiny
straight stitches.

Form the three pansies and attach
each one over the leaves in the same
manner. Work a loose French knot in the
centre of each one.

### Medium roses

Fashion four folded ribbon roses and stitch them between the pansies. Using the 4mm (³⁄₁₆") green silk ribbon, work tiny ribbon stitch leaves around the folded roses.

### Rosebuds

Embroider the rosebuds around the design with a straight stitch or a pair of slightly overlapping straight stitches. Using the green thread, stitch a fly stitch with a long anchoring stitch for the calyx on each bud. Stitch a tiny horizontal straight stitch across the base of the 'V' on the fly stitch (*diag 1*).

*Diag 1*

### Small buds and scattered leaves

Randomly work the French knot buds next, making some a little larger than others by varying the tension on the ribbon.

Fill in the spaces around the design with more tiny ribbon stitch leaves and the crystal beads.

## Embroidery key

*All thread embroidery is worked with one strand unless otherwise specified.*

### Large central roses

Petals = D and F, or E and F (loop stitch)
Centre = I (beading)
Leaves = G (ribbon stitch)

### Pansies

Petals = C and E, or D and E (gathering)
Centre = F (colonial knot)
Leaves = G (gathering)

*Medium roses* = E (folded ribbon rose)

### Rosebuds

Petals = E (straight stitch)
Calyx = A (fly stitch, straight stitch)
Leaves = B (ribbon stitch)

### Small buds

Buds = C, D, E and F (colonial knot), H (beading)
Leaves = B (ribbon stitch)

# GATHERED RIBBON LEAF

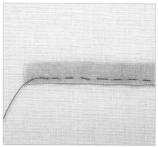

1 Cut a 6cm (2 ³⁄₈") length of ribbon. Using matching thread, knot the end. Work running stitch along one edge. Leave needle dangling.

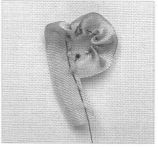

2 Pull up the running stitches, folding the ribbon in half with the gathers along the centre.

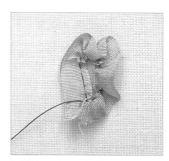

3 Using tiny stitches catch the two ends of ribbon together.

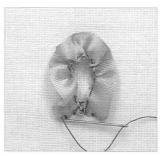

4 Place the ribbon onto the fabric. Tuck under the raw ends and secure.

5 Secure the sides in the same manner, making a fold at the tip. Catch the tip in place. **Completed gathered ribbon leaf.**

# PANSY

The petals of this delightful flower are assembled before the pansy is attached to the fabric. Two different colours of ribbon are used.

**1 Upper petals.** Cut a 7cm (2 ¾") piece of ribbon. Fold the ribbon at right angles across the centre. Pin.

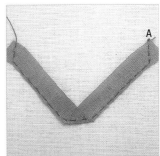

**2** Secure the thread at A. Work running stitches across the corners and along the edges as shown.

**3** Pull up the running stitches so the stitches form a slight arc with a pointed tail at the centre. Back stitch to secure the thread.

**4 Middle and lower petals.** Cut a 7cm (2 ¾") length of ribbon. Fold into thirds and mark each fold with a pin.

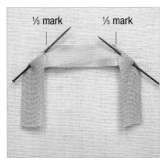

**5** Refold the ribbon as shown. Pin the diagonal folds.

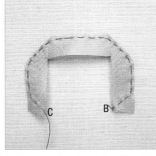

**6** Secure the thread at B with a knot. Work running stitches across the corners and along the edges as shown until reaching C.

**7** Pull up the running stitches tightly, forming three petals. Back stitch to secure. Take a stitch from B to C forming a circle in the centre.

**8** Using the same thread, attach these petals to the upper petals. Ensure the upper petals sit well above the middle petals.

**9** Secure the pansy to the fabric with tiny stab stitches around the centre hole.

**10** End off the thread. Using ribbon, work a colonial knot at the centre.
**Completed pansy.**

# HEART

## by Kris Richards

### This design uses

*Beading, Detached chain, Ribbon stitch, Stem stitch*

### Ribbon embroidery index

Detached chain 12
Ribbon stitch 23

## Materials

### Threads, ribbons & beads

*DMC stranded cotton*
A = 3012 med khaki green
B = 3023 lt Jacobean green
*YLI silk ribbon 7mm (⁵⁄₁₆") wide*
C = 30cm (12") no. 162 pale mushroom
D = 30cm (12") no. 178 lt antique violet
*YLI silk ribbon 4mm (³⁄₁₆") wide*
E = 50cm (20") no. 56 med olive green

F = 50cm (20") no. 163 med dusky pink
*Kacoonda hand dyed silk ribbon 4mm (³⁄₁₆") wide*
G = 30cm (12") no. 107 soft sage
*Mill Hill glass seed beads*
H = 00123 cream
*Mill Hill antique glass beads*
I = 03051 misty

### Needles

No. 9 crewel needle
No. 18 chenille needle
No. 22 chenille needle

## Order of work

Use the no. 22 chenille needle for the 4mm (³⁄₁₆") ribbon and the no. 18 chenille needle for the 7mm (⁵⁄₁₆") ribbon. The crewel needle is used for the thread embroidery and for attaching the beads.

### Flowers

Embroider the petals of the flowers first, working nine ribbon stitches for the petals of each pink flower and five ribbon stitches for the petals of each mushroom and violet flower. Secure a bead to the centre of each one.

### Stems and leaves

Stitch all ribbon leaves next. Using the Jacobean green thread, stitch the stems along the upper section of the heart. Scatter detached chain leaves around the pink flowers and at the tips of the stems. Change to the khaki green thread and work the stems and small leaves in the lower half of the design in a similar manner.

### Embroidery key

*All thread embroidery is worked with one strand.*

#### Pink flowers

Petals = F (ribbon stitch)
Centre = I (beading)
Leaves = G (ribbon stitch), B (detached chain)

#### Mushroom and violet flowers

Petals = C or D (ribbon stitch)
Centre = H (beading)
Leaves = E (ribbon stitch, detached chain), A (detached chain)

#### Heart outline

Upper stems = B (stem stitch)
Leaves on upper stems = B (detached chain)
Lower stems = A (stem stitch)
Leaves on lower stems = A (detached chain)

# VICTORIAN BOUQUET

## by Libby Vater

### This design uses

*Beading, Bullion knot, Couching, Detached chain, Fly stitch, Folded ribbon rose, Gathering, Grab stitch, Loop stitch, Ribbon stitch, Rolled ribbon rose variation, Satin stitch, Straight stitch*

### Ribbon embroidery index

Blossom bud 80
Folded ribbon rose 14
Gathered ribbon blossom 17
Grab stitch 19
Loop stitch 19
Ribbon stitch 23

## Materials

*Threads, ribbons & beads*

Machine sewing threads to match ribbons
*Anchor stranded cotton*
A = 262 dk pine green
B = 263 vy dk pine green
C = 859 fern green
*Gumnut Yarns 'Stars' stranded silk*
D = 173 vy lt mulberry
E = 176 med mulberry
*Rajmahal Art silk*
F = 841 gilded bronze

*Hanah hand dyed bias cut silk ribbon 15mm (⅝") wide*
G = 1.5m (1yd 23") blushing bride
H = 50cm (20") earth mother
*Hanah hand dyed bias cut silk ribbon 25mm (1") wide*
I = 1.5m (1yd 23") lingerie
*Mokuba no. 1520 gold edged organdy ribbon 15mm (⅝") wide*
J = 50cm (20") no. 36 dk avocado green
*Glen Lorin hand dyed silk ribbon 4mm (³⁄₁₆") wide*
K = 1m (39 ½") grace
*Glen Lorin hand dyed silk ribbon 7mm (⁵⁄₁₆") wide*
L = 1.5m (1yd 23") green sands
*Petals hand dyed silk ribbon 7mm (⁵⁄₁₆") wide*
M = 2m (2yd 7") rose gold
*The Thread Gatherer Silken Ribbons silk ribbon 7mm (⁵⁄₁₆") wide*
N = 80cm (31 ½") no. SR7 057 English meadow
*Mill Hill glass seed beads*
O = 00557 gold
*Mill Hill petite glass beads*
P = 42027 champagne
*Gütermann 6mm (¼") beads*
Q = 2885 gold

## Needles

No. 9 straw (milliner's) needle
No. 10 crewel needle
No. 18 chenille needle
Fine beading needle

## Supplies

Soft gold twisted cord

## Order of work

Use the no. 18 chenille needle for the ribbon and gold cord. Use the beading needle for the beading and the straw needle for the bullion knots. The crewel needle is used for all other thread embroidery.

### Main stems and long leaves

Embroider the stems, using satin stitch worked at an angle. Stitch the elongated leaves peeping from the edges of the posy in the same manner, changing the stitch direction at the folds.

Using the gold cord, work two bands of straight stitches across the main stems.

### Large roses

Dye the ribbon for the large roses in a cup of black tea. Allow to dry.

Make six folded ribbon roses. Vary the size of each rose slightly. Secure the roses to the fabric with matching machine sewing thread.

### Small roses

Work seven folded ribbon roses in a similar manner to the large roses, making the centres firmer and the petals a little less open.

### Large blossoms

Cut a 21cm (8 ¼") length of ribbon for each of the three large blossoms. Fold the pieces in half along the length and press. Work a row of gathering stitches on each piece of ribbon *(diag 1)*.

Pull up the gathering threads to form the petals. Secure the flowers to the fabric. Attach three gold beads in the centre and then add eight to ten champagne beads around them.

### Blossom buds

Make six buds following the step-by-step instructions. Using matching machine thread, stitch them in place around the outer edge of the design. Work a grab stitch across the base of each bud, finishing with a long anchoring stitch.

### Lavender

Embroider a bullion knot for each head of lavender and add a long straight stitch at the tip of each knot. For the calyx and stem of each flower head, work a fly stitch with a long anchoring stitch. Couch the longer stems to form a bend.

### Blue buds

Starting some at the tip, work a loose ribbon stitch for each bud. Add a grab stitch with a long anchoring stitch for the calyx and stem of each bud. Work extra straight stitches on the ends of some stems to form the bend. Stitch detached chain leaves.

### Burgundy sprays

Embroider loop stitches approximately 7mm (⁵⁄₁₆") long for the flowers. Work a straight stitch over the lower half of each loop for the calyx and then a long straight stitch for each stem.

### Foliage and beads

Fill any spaces among the large roses and blossoms with loop stitches. Using the narrower green ribbon, work ribbon stitch leaves around the outer edge of the posy. Embroider single or pairs of detached chain leaves around the outer edge. Attach the large gold beads among the roses and blooms.

*Diag 1*

## Embroidery key

*All thread embroidery is worked with one strand unless otherwise specified.*

*Main stems and long leaves* = A and B (satin stitch)

*Gold band* = gold twisted cord (straight stitch)

*Large roses* = G (folded ribbon rose)

*Large blossoms*
Petals = I (gathering)
Centre = O and P (beading)

*Small roses* = M (folded ribbon rose)

*Blossom buds*
Petals = I (rolled ribbon rosebud variation)
Calyx = L (grab stitch)

*Lavender*
Flowers = D and E (bullion knot, 11–12 wraps, straight stitch)
Stems = C (fly stitch, couching)

*Blue buds*
Petals = N (ribbon stitch)
Calyx = C (fly stitch)

*Stems* = C (straight stitch)
*Leaves* = C (detached chain)

*Burgundy sprays*
Flowers = K (loop stitch)
Calyx and stems = C (straight stitch)

*Foliage and beads*
Loops among roses and blossoms = H, J and N (loop stitch)
Outer leaves = L (ribbon stitch), F (2 strands, detached chain)
Beads = Q (beading)

# BLOSSOM BUD

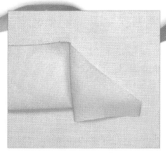

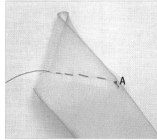

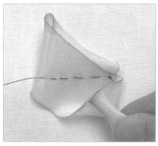

1 Fold a 90° angle in the right hand end of the ribbon, bringing the end 2mm (⅛") below the lower edge.

2 Fold the left hand end of the ribbon, bringing the upper edge to meet the angled fold on the right, forming a cone shape.

3 Secure a length of thread at A. Stitch a row of gathering through the two front layers of the ribbon. Do not catch the back edge.

4 Fold the tail end of ribbon in half along the length and roll up tightly.

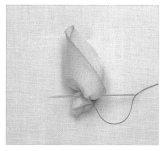

5 Twist the roll and turn it up and into the cone of ribbon. Ensure the folded end is inserted first.

6 Holding the roll in place, continue stitching the row of gathering along the lower back edge of the cone.

7 Pull up the gathering thread firmly. Secure the rolled centre and base of the bud through all layers with several back stitches.

8 **Completed blossom bud.**

# WINTER GARLAND
## by Beverley Gogel

### Flowers

Work eight flowers, arranging them into a circlet. Slightly overlap the petals of the previous flower. For each flower leave a small space in the centre and work six loop stitches approximately 1cm (⅜") long in a circle for the petals. Stitch a gold straight stitch along the base of each petal for the highlights. Add a loose colonial knot for each centre.

### Foliage

Embroider pairs of detached chain leaves between the flowers on the outer edge of the circlet. Stitch one light green and one dark green leaf for each pair.

### This design uses

*Colonial knot, Detached chain, Loop stitch, Straight stitch*

#### Ribbon embroidery index

Colonial knot 9
Detached chain 12
Loop stitch 19
Loop stitch flower 21

## Materials

### Thread & ribbons

*Au Papillon metallic thread*
A = col. A, bright gold
*YLI silk ribbon 4mm (³/₁₆") wide*
B = 40cm (16") no. 56 med olive green
C = 40cm (16") no. 171 avocado green
*YLI silk ribbon 7mm (⁵/₁₆") wide*
D = 30cm (12") no. 156 cream
*Kacoonda hand dyed silk ribbon 7mm (⁵/₁₆") wide*
E = 60cm (24") no. 15 lt dusky rose
F = 20cm (8") no. 16 lemon fizz
G = 30cm (12") no. 102 winter morning
H = 20cm (8") no. 103 golden sunset
I = 60cm (24") no. 105 copper rose
J = 60cm (24") no. 109 mulberry

### Needles

No. 9 straw (milliner's) needle
No. 20 chenille needle

## Order of work

Use the photograph as a guide for ribbon colour changes within the design.

The chenille needle is used for the ribbon embroidery and the straw needle is used when stitching with the gold metallic thread.

## Embroidery key

*All thread embroidery is worked with three strands.*

### Plum flowers

Petals = J (loop stitch)
Highlights = A (straight stitch)
Centre = F (colonial knot)

### Copper flowers

Petals = I (loop stitch)
Highlights = A (straight stitch)
Centre = F (colonial knot)

### Pink flowers

Petals = E (loop stitch)
Highlights = A (straight stitch)
Centre = H (colonial knot)

### Cream flowers

Petals = D and G (loop stitch)
Highlights = A (straight stitch)
Centre = H (colonial knot)

*Leaves* = B and C (detached chain)

# NASTURTIUMS

## by Cathy Veide

### This design uses

*Bullion knot, French knot, Loop stitch, Looped straight stitch, Padded straight stitch, Stem stitch, Straight stitch*

### Ribbon embroidery index

French knot 16
Loop stitch 19
Looped straight stitch 33
Padded straight stitch 34
Straight stitch 33

### Materials

#### Threads & ribbons

*DMC stranded cotton*
A = 725 dk golden yellow
B = 817 vy dk coral red
C = 902 maroon
D = 3052 med green-grey
E = 3348 lt yellow-green
*Bucilla variegated silk ribbon 13mm (½") wide*
F = 20cm (8") no. 2-1311 olive greens
*Bucilla silk ribbon 7mm (⁵⁄₁₆") wide*
G = 20cm (8") no. 27-522 orange
H = 20cm (8") no. 666 sunflower yellow
I = 15cm (6") no. 27-020 fern green
*Bucilla silk ribbon 4mm (³⁄₁₆") wide*
J = 20cm (8") no. 512 deep orange
K = 20cm (8") no. 666 sunflower yellow
L = 20cm (8") no. 24-642 lt emerald

### Needles

No. 8 crewel needle
No. 9 straw (milliner's) needle
No. 20 chenille needle
No. 22 chenille needle
No. 24 chenille needle
Tapestry needle

### Order of work

Use the no. 20 chenille needle for the 13mm (½") ribbon, the no. 22 chenille needle for the 7mm (⁵⁄₁₆") ribbon and the no. 24 chenille needle when stitching with the 4mm (³⁄₁₆") ribbon. Work the bullion knot with the straw needle and all other thread embroidery using the crewel needle. The tapestry needle is used for shaping some stitches.

### Stems, leaves and buds

Embroider the stems first, using two strands of thread for the lower sections and one strand of thread for the upper sections.

Place a green French knot bud at the tip of the tallest stem. Add four small leaves along the stem. Work a looped straight stitch for the medium leaf, forming it into an oval shape with a tapestry needle. Stitch three radiating straight stitches to anchor the centre of the leaf and form the leaf veins. Embroider the two large leaves in the same manner, using four straight stitches for the leaf veins on each one.

Stitch two straight stitches, one on top of the other, for the yellow bud. Add a bullion knot for the 'tail' of the bud.

### Flowers

Work the orange flowers next, beginning with two loop stitches for the upper petals. Stitch the lower petals with looped straight stitches. Use the tapestry needle to shape and plump up the stitches. Add five radiating straight stitches over the upper petals for markings.

Embroider the petals of the yellow flower in the same manner. Work a group of three straight stitches in a fan shape on each upper petal.

Finish the lower orange and yellow flowers with two French knots in the centre of each one.

# RED ROSES

## by Angela Dower

### This design uses

*Folded ribbon rose – spider web rose combination, Fly stitch, Looped ribbon stitch, Ribbon stitch, Side ribbon stitch, Stem stitch, Straight stitch, Twisted detached chain*

### Ribbon embroidery index

Folded ribbon rose – spider web rose combination 85
Looped ribbon stitch 25
Ribbon stitch 23
Side ribbon stitch 26
Straight stitch 33
Twisted detached chain 13

## Materials

### Threads & ribbons

Machine sewing thread to match red ribbon
*Kacoonda fine silk*
A = 8E lt olive
*YLI silk floss*
B = 157 drab olive
*Kacoonda hand dyed silk ribbon 4mm (³⁄₁₆") wide*
C = 1m (39 ½") no. 8E lt olive
*YLI silk ribbon 4mm (³⁄₁₆") wide*
D = 50cm (20") no. 171 dk avocado green
*Glen Lorin hand dyed silk ribbon 4mm (³⁄₁₆") wide*
E = 1m (39 ½") telepea
*YLI silk ribbon 7mm (⁵⁄₁₆") wide*
F = 1m (39 ½") no. 50 dk scarlet

### Needles

No. 9 straw (milliner's) needle
No. 18 chenille needle
No. 22 chenille needle
No. 20 tapestry needle

### Supplies

Dressmaker's awl

## Order of work

Use the no. 22 chenille needle for the 4mm (³⁄₁₆") ribbon, the no. 18 chenille needle for the 7mm (⁵⁄₁₆") ribbon and the no. 20 tapestry needle for inserting the rose centres. The no. 9 straw needle is used for all thread embroidery.

### Main stems

Embroider the main stems for the roses and leaves in stem stitch.

### Large roses

Stitch the three large ribbon roses following the step-by-step instructions.

### Side view roses

To stitch the lower rose, work a twisted detached chain for the centre with the scarlet ribbon. Using the darker sections of E, work a side ribbon stitch on each side of the centre for the back petals. Using the lighter sections, work three ribbon stitches for the side petals and front petal.

Embroider the upper rose in the same manner as before, adding a looped ribbon stitch at the base of the flower for the curled petal.

Stitch a tiny straight stitch in ribbon across the base of each flower to begin the calyx. Change to thread and add a straight stitch on each side of the previous stitch.

### Rosebuds

Stitch a twisted detached chain for the centre of each large bud. Add a side ribbon stitch to each side of the centre, crossing the stitches over at the base. Stitch the calyx in the same manner as those on the side view roses.

Work the petals of the small bud with a twisted detached chain. For the calyx, work a straight stitch along each side of the bud, overlapping them at the base. Add a tiny straight stitch across the end of the previous two straight stitches.

For the tiny green bud at the tip of the sprig, work two straight stitches, one on top of the other. Embroider a fly stitch at the tip and a tiny straight stitch across the base.

### Leaves and leaf stems

Embroider the leaves in ribbon stitch, using both shades of green ribbon. Work a tiny straight stitch at the end of each leaf to attach it to the main stem.

## Embroidery key

*All thread embroidery is worked with one strand.*

*Main stems* = A (stem stitch)

### Large roses

Centre = F (folded ribbon rose)
Petals = E (spider web rose)

### Side view roses

Centre = F (twisted detached chain)
Back petals = F (side ribbon stitch)
Side and front petals = E (ribbon stitch)
Curled petal = E (looped ribbon stitch) or none
Calyx = A and D (straight stitch)

### Large buds

Centre = F (twisted detached chain)
Petals = E (ribbon stitch)
Calyx = A and D (straight stitch)

### Small bud

Petals = F (twisted detached chain)
Calyx = C (straight stitch)

### Green bud

Calyx = D (straight stitch)
Tip = B (fly stitch)

### Leaves and leaf stems

Leaves = C and D (ribbon stitch)
Leaf stems = B (straight stitch)

*Symphony of Flowers*

# FOLDED RIBBON ROSE – SPIDER WEB ROSE COMBINATION

The realism of these roses is created by combining two ribbon embroidery techniques–folding and weaving. To add to the realistic effect, use the darker sections of the shaded ribbon near the centre and the lighter sections around the outer edge.

**1 Centre.** Make a folded ribbon rose approx 8mm (⁵⁄₁₆") in diameter, following steps 1–8 on page 14.

**2** To end off, wind the thread around the base of the rose centre and stitch to the tail of ribbon. Leave ribbon tail and thread dangling.

**3 Framework for outer petals.** Using matching thread, work five evenly spaced straight stitch spokes leaving a small space in the centre.

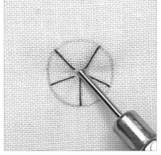

**4 Inserting centre.** Using the dressmaker's awl, make a hole in the centre of the framework.

Wrong side of fabric

**5** Using the tapestry needle, insert the tails of ribbon and thread of the folded ribbon rose through the hole. Secure the tails on the back.

**6 Outer petals.** Change ribbon. Bring the ribbon to the front under the folded ribbon rose between two spokes.

**7** Twist the ribbon once and take it over the next spoke in an anti-clockwise direction.

**8** Make a twist in the ribbon again and take the needle under the next spoke.

**9** Weave around the circle forming a twist in the ribbon between each spoke.

**10** Continue weaving until the spokes are covered. Take the ribbon to the back and secure. **Completed rose.**

# FLORAL CORONET

## by Jan Kerton

### This design uses

*Beading, Detached chain, Fly stitch,
French knot, Loop stitch, Ribbon stitch,
Spider web rose, Straight stitch*

### Ribbon embroidery index

Detached chain 12
French knot 16
Loop stitch 19
Loop stitch flower 21
Ribbon stitch 23
Single loop stitch flower 20
Spider web rose 30
Straight stitch 33

## Materials

### Threads, ribbons & beads

*Madeira stranded silk*
A = 1701 vy lt blue-green
B = 2207 vy lt old gold
*YLI silk ribbon 4mm (³⁄₁₆") wide*
C = 1m (39 ½") no. 1 white
D = 1.5m (1yd 23") no. 5 blush pink
E = 1m (39 ½") no. 13 lt yellow
F = 1.5m (1yd 23") no. 90 vy lt
antique blue
G = 1m (39 ½") no. 100 lt blue-violet
H = 1m (39 ½") no. 154 lichen green
I = 1.5m (1yd 23") no. 156 cream
*Mill Hill glass seed beads*
J = 02002 yellow creme

### Needles

No. 8 crewel needle
No. 22 chenille needle

## Order of work

Use the no. 8 crewel needle when
working with the silk thread and
attaching the beads and the no. 22
chenille needle for the silk ribbon.

### Pink anemones and buds

Embroider four pairs of flowers around
the design, working five loop stitch
petals for each flower. Secure each petal
with a tiny straight stitch over the base
using the old gold silk thread. Attach a
bead to the centre of each flower.

Stitch the buds in groups of two or
three around the design. Work the petals
with two tiny straight stitches, one on
top of the other.

Changing to the green silk thread,
stitch a fly stitch around the bud for the
calyx and a straight stitch over the base
of each bud. Work a tiny straight stitch
at the tip of most of the petals.

### Yellow roses and buds

Embroider seven large and four small
spider web roses. Stitch a framework of
five straight stitch spokes using the old
gold silk thread.

Use the yellow silk ribbon for the
inner rounds of weaving and the cream
ribbon for the outer rounds. Stitch the
buds in the same manner as the
pink buds.

### Lavender

Work three or four detached chain
stitches for each bunch of lavender.

### Forget-me-nots

Embroider the forget-me-nots around
the design singly or in groups of two or
three. Each forget-me-not is worked
with a French knot for the centre.
Surround this with five French knots for
the petals.

### White blossom

Fill in around the design with tiny single
loop stitch flowers, varying the sizes.
Flatten the loop and work a yellow
French knot for the centre.

### Leaves

Using the green silk ribbon, scatter tiny
ribbon stitch leaves around the inner
and outer edges of the coronet.

## Embroidery key

*All thread embroidery is worked with
one strand.*

### Pink anemones and buds

Petals = D (loop stitch)
Petal markings = B (straight stitch)
Centre = J and B (beading)
Bud petals = D (straight stitch)
Bud calyxes = A (fly stitch,
straight stitch)

### Yellow roses and buds

Framework = B (straight stitch)
Inner petals = E (spider web rose)
Outer petals = I (spider web rose)
Bud petals = I (straight stitch)
Bud calyxes = A (fly stitch,
straight stitch)

*Lavender* = G (detached chain)

### Forget-me-nots

Petals = F (French knot, 1 wrap)
Centre = E (French knot, 1 wrap)

### White blossom

Petals = C (loop stitch)
Centre = B (French knot, 2 wraps)

*Leaves* = H (ribbon stitch)

*Tara*

# COTTAGE GARDEN

## by Shirley Sinclair

### This design uses

*Colonial knot, Feather stitch, Ribbon stitch,*
*Rolled ribbon, Straight stitch,*
*Whipped chain stitch*

### Ribbon embroidery index

Colonial knot 9
Detached daisy 90
Ribbon stitch 23
Straight stitch 33

## Materials

### Threads & ribbons

Dark green machine sewing thread
*DMC stranded cotton*
A = 938 ultra dk coffee brown
B = 3362 dk pine green
*Madeira stranded cotton*
C = 1510 lt green-grey
D = 2206 med lt old gold
E = 2403 cream
*Kacoonda hand dyed 2 ply silk*
F = 306 autumn green
*YLI silk ribbon 2mm (⅛") wide*
G = 2m (2yd 7") no. 3 white
H = 1m (39 ½") no. 126 periwinkle blue
*YLI silk ribbon 4mm (³⁄₁₆") wide*
I = 80cm (31 ½") no. 1 antique white
J = 30cm (12") no. 13 vy lt yellow
K = 30cm (12") no. 14 lt yellow
L = 60cm (24") no. 20 forest green
M = 40cm (16") no. 177 antique mauve
*YLI silk ribbon 7mm (⁵⁄₁₆") wide*
N = 30cm (12") no. 20 forest green

## Needles

No. 8 crewel needle
No. 20 chenille needle
No. 22 tapestry needle

### Supplies

Water soluble fabric (eg *Solvy*)

## Order of work

Use the chenille needle for all ribbon
embroidery, the tapestry needle for the
whipped chain stitch and the crewel
needle for all other thread embroidery.

### Stems and twigs

With the exception of the detached
daisies, embroider the main stems for
the daisies in whipped chain stitch.
Work the side stems and twigs with
feather stitch and straight stitch.

## Daisies

Embroider the two large facing daisies first. Using the antique white silk ribbon, work four to eight random ribbon stitches for the underlying petals. Change to the white silk ribbon and work the upper layer of petals, partially covering the petals underneath.

Stitch the side view daisy on the upper left in the same manner. Work the yellow side view daisy with a single layer of petals.

Work the two daisy buds with five or six ribbon stitches using the white silk ribbon. Add a calyx of four to five straight stitches at the base of each one.

Embroider the two detached daisies following the step-by-step instructions. Make the first daisy with ten petals and the second daisy with nine.

Fill the centres of the daisies with colonial knots, using the photograph as a guide for colour changes.

Attach the daisies to the design with tiny back stitches through the green ribbon stalk.

## Heartsease

The detached heartsease are also worked on the water soluble fabric.

Lay a 15mm (⅝") piece of forest green ribbon horizontally onto the water soluble fabric. This is the foundation for the petals. Embroider the lower petals first, using the light yellow ribbon, working them onto the green ribbon. Stitch the three upper petals to the ribbon, in the same manner. Work a colonial knot for the centre.

Using the coffee brown thread, stitch four tiny straight stitches radiating from the centre over the lower two petals.

Dissolve the water soluble fabric and attach each flower to the design in the same manner as the detached daisies.

## Forget-me-nots

Using the photograph as a guide, work the ten forget-me-nots along the base of the design. Stitch a colonial knot for the centre of each flower using the bright yellow silk ribbon. Work five periwinkle blue French knots for the petals.

## Leaves

Stitch the leaves for the forget-me-nots and some of the daisies in ribbon stitch.

# Embroidery key

*All thread embroidery is worked with one strand unless otherwise specified.*

## Stems and twigs

Main stems = F (whipped chain stitch)
Side stems and twigs = F (feather stitch, straight stitch)

## Facing daisies

Under petals = I (ribbon stitch)
Over petals = G (ribbon stitch)
Centre = D and E (2 strands, colonial knot)

## Side view daisy on left

Under petals = I (ribbon stitch)
Over petals = G (ribbon stitch)
Centre = C (2 strands, colonial knot)

## Side view daisy on right

Petals = J (ribbon stitch)
Centre = D (2 strands, colonial knot)

## Detached daisies

Petals = I (ribbon stitch)
Centre = C (2 strands, colonial knot), B (colonial knot)
Stalk = N (rolled ribbon)

## Daisy buds

Petals = I (ribbon stitch)
Calyx = F (straight stitch)

## Heartsease

Foundation = N (straight stitch)
Lower petals = K (ribbon stitch)
Upper petals = M (ribbon stitch)
Centre = D (colonial knot), A (straight stitch)

## Forget-me-nots

Petals = H (colonial knot)
Centre = D (colonial knot)

Leaves = L (ribbon stitch)

*Earthly Possessions*

# DETACHED DAISY

1  Place the water soluble fabric in a hoop. Lay the ribbon across the fabric for the width of the centre plus the length of the first petal.

2  **Petal.** Take the needle through the ribbon approx 13mm (½") from the end of the ribbon. This will be the tip of the petal.

3  Pull ribbon through gently, to form the first petal. Bring needle to the front through the tail of the ribbon approx 5mm (³⁄₁₆") from the end.

4  Pull the ribbon through. Lay the ribbon out flat for the second petal. Take the needle to the back through the ribbon at the tip.

5  Pull the ribbon through.

6  Continue working petals, leaving an oval shape in the centre. End off on the back with 2–3 tiny stitches in matching thread.

7  **Centre.** Work 4–10 colonial knots in the oval shape.

8  Cut away the excess fabric. Soak the flower in water for a few minutes and then leave to dry.

9  **Stalk.** Roll up 15mm (⅝") of green ribbon and secure to the back of the daisy with 2–3 tiny back stitches.

10  **Completed daisy.**

# KNOT FLOWERS

## by Beverley Gogel

### This design uses

*Colonial knot, French knot, Grab stitch, Ribbon stitch, Straight stitch*

#### Ribbon embroidery index

Colonial knot 9
Ribbon stitch 23

## Materials

### Threads & ribbons

*DMC stranded cotton*
A = 732 olive green
B = 733 med olive green
C = 734 lt olive green
D = 3708 lt melon
E = 3854 med autumn gold
F = 3856 ultra vy lt mahogany
*YLI silk ribbon 7mm (⁵⁄₁₆") wide*
G = 40cm (16") no. 56 med olive green

*Kacoonda hand dyed silk ribbon 13mm (½") wide*
H = 1.5m (1yd 23") no. 6F coral rose
I = 1.5m (1yd 23") no. 103 golden sunset

### Needles

No. 1 straw (milliner's) needle
No. 5 straw (milliner's) needle
No. 13 chenille needle
No. 22 chenille needle

## Order of work

Use the no.13 chenille needle for the 13mm (½") ribbon and the no.22 chenille needle for the 7mm (⁵⁄₁₆") ribbon. Embroider all French knots with the no. 1 straw needle and the remaining thread embroidery with the no. 5 straw needle.

### Flowers

Both flowers are embroidered in the same manner. Draw a circle, 16mm (⁵⁄₈") in diameter, for the centre of the flower. Surround the circle with a row of closely worked colonial knots. Fill the centre with tightly packed French knots. Where two thread colours are used for the knots, ensure the colours are evenly mixed throughout the centre.

### Foliage

Work a long loose straight stitch for the stem. Add a pair of ribbon stitch leaves, one on each side of the stem. Anchor each leaf to the stem with a grab stitch.

## Embroidery key

*All thread embroidery is worked with one strand unless otherwise specified.*

### Bright pink flower

Petals = H (colonial knot)
Centre = D (6 strands, French knot, 1 wrap)

### Gold flower

Petals = I (colonial knot)
Centre = E and F (6 strands, French knot, 1 wrap)

### Foliage

Stem = A, B and C blended together (1 strand of each, straight stitch)
Leaves = G (ribbon stitch)
Base of leaf = A, B and C blended together (1 strand of each, grab stitch)

# DESPREZ À FLEUR

by Lynda Maker

## This design uses

*Beading, Couching, Folded ribbon stitch,*
*French knot, Fishbone stitch,*
*Gathered ribbon rose, Looped ribbon stitch,*
*Ribbon stitch, Side ribbon stitch,*
*Split back stitch, Straight stitch, Tied ribbon*

## Ribbon embroidery index

Couching 11
Folded ribbon stitch 24
Gathered ribbon rose 18
Looped ribbon stitch 25
Padded rosebud 94
Ribbon stitch 23
Side ribbon stitch 26
Straight stitch 33

## Materials

### Threads, ribbons & beads

*Madeira stranded silk*
A = 2211 med topaz
*Gumnut Yarns 'Stars' shaded silk*
B = 645 med khaki
C = 677 olive
*YLI silk ribbon 4mm (³⁄₁₆") wide*
D = 4m (4yd 14") no. 56 med
olive green
E = 40cm (16") no. 71 ultra lt
canary yellow
*YLI silk ribbon 7mm (⁵⁄₁₆") wide*
F = 1.5m (1yd 23") no. 14 lt yellow
G = 2m (2yd 7") no. 56 med olive green
H = 1m (39 ½") no. 72 dk olive green
*YLI silk ribbon 13mm (½") wide*
I = 1.2m (1yd 12") no. 156 cream
*Mokuba rayon ribbon 8mm (⁵⁄₁₆") wide*
J = 70cm (28") no. 15 gold
*Mill Hill glass seed beads*
K = 02019 crystal honey

### Needles

No. 10 crewel needle
No. 13 chenille needle
No. 18 chenille needle
No. 22 chenille needle
Fine beading needle

### Supplies

7 × 7mm (⁵⁄₁₆") round beads for
padding buds
Yellow silk paint

## Order of work

Use the no. 13 chenille needle for the
13mm (½") ribbon, the no. 18 chenille
needle for the 7mm (⁵⁄₁₆") ribbon and the
no. 22 chenille needle for the 4mm (³⁄₁₆")
ribbon. The crewel needle is used for all
thread embroidery and the beading
needle for attaching the beads.

### Leaves, stems and beads

Use the photograph as a guide for
thread colour changes within the design.
Embroider the groups of thread leaves in
fishbone stitch, using the shaded
silk threads.
   Work the large ribbon leaves next.
Stitch the stems in split back stitch and
add the tiny ribbon stitch leaves.
Randomly secure glass seed beads at the
ends of the stems either singly or in
groups of two to five.

### Roses

Using the wide pale yellow ribbon, work
the three large gathered roses. Dilute the
yellow silk paint and tint the ribbon in
the centre of the roses. When completely
dry, stitch clusters of topaz French knots
in the centre of each one.

### Rosebuds

Stitch the large beads in pairs or a group
of three around the gathered roses.
Using the light yellow and yellow-beige
ribbons, cover each bead following the
step-by-step instructions. Embroider the
calyxes around the buds using both
widths of the olive green ribbon.

### Bow

Tie the gold ribbon into a bow with bow
loops approximately 2.5cm (1") long.
Stitch the bow just below the roses with
two or three tiny stitches.
   Gently fold the tails to give the effect
of flowing and catch the edge of the
ribbon folds to the fabric with tiny
straight stitches.

## Embroidery key

*All thread embroidery is worked with
two strands unless otherwise specified.*

### Roses

Petals = I (gathering)
Centres = A (French knot, 1 wrap)

### Rosebuds

Petals = E and F, or F (ribbon stitch)
Calyxes = D (ribbon stitch)

### Leaves, stems and beads

Thread leaves = B or C
(fishbone stitch)
Large ribbon leaves = G and H
(looped ribbon stitch, side ribbon
stitch, folded ribbon stitch,
straight stitch)
Stems = B (split back stitch)
Tiny leaves = D (ribbon stitch, side
ribbon stitch)
Beads = K (beading)
Bow = J (tied ribbon, couching)

*Heart Strings*

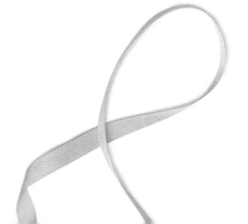

# PADDED ROSEBUD

1 Secure a large bead to the fabric. Pass the thread through the bead twice to hold it firm.

2 **Inner petals.** Using the 7mm (⁵⁄₁₆") ribbon, bring it to the front of the fabric 4mm (³⁄₁₆") away from the bead (A).

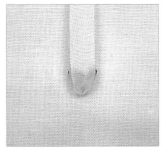

3 Lay the ribbon over the bead, ensuring it is smooth and spread as wide as possible.

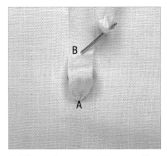

4 Place the tip of the needle onto the centre of the ribbon 3mm (¹⁄₈") away from the bead (B).

5 Place your thumb on the bead and pull the ribbon through to form a ribbon stitch (thumb not shown).

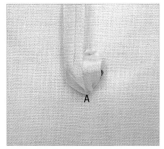

6 Bring the ribbon to the front as close as possible to A. Lay the ribbon along one side of the bead, overlapping the first stitch.

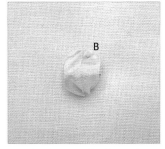

7 Take the needle through the ribbon and to the back of the fabric just beyond B.

8 Repeat steps 6 and 7 on the other side of the bead.

9 **Outer petals.** Change to the 4mm (³⁄₁₆") ribbon. Work a ribbon stitch along one side, starting and ending close to the previous stitches.

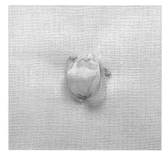

10 Work a ribbon stitch on the other side, finishing approx three quarters of the way along the bud.

11 **Calyx.** Change ribbon. Beginning just below the base of the petals, work a ribbon stitch along one side of the bud.

12 Work a ribbon stitch, in the same manner, on the other side. Secure any tails of ribbon on the back. **Completed rosebud.**

# SNOWDROPS

## by Helen Eriksson

### This design uses

*Detached chain, Folded ribbon stitch, French knot, Ribbon stitch, Stem stitch, Straight stitch*

### Ribbon embroidery index

Detached chain 12
Folded ribbon stitch 24
Ribbon stitch 23
Straight stitch 33

## Materials

### Thread & ribbons

*Anchor stranded cotton*
A = 269 ultra dk avocado green
*YLI silk ribbon 4mm (³/₁₆") wide*
B = 1m (39 ½") no. 3 white
C = 1m (39 ½") no. 21 dk forest green
D = 20cm (8") no. 56 med olive green

### Needles

No. 8 crewel needle
No. 20 chenille needle

## Order of work

Use the chenille needle for the ribbon embroidery and the crewel needle for the thread embroidery.

### Flowers

Stitch three downward facing detached chains for the petals of the five flowers. For each flower, begin the stitches at the same position on the fabric and fan them out slightly.

   Add each calyx with tiny straight stitches. Using the thread, stitch the spots at the tips of the petals with French knots.

### Buds

Stitch the petals and calyxes of the three buds in the same manner as the flowers, but use only two detached chains for the petals of each one.

### Stems

Embroider the stems for the flowers and buds with stem stitch. Begin each one at the calyx and work towards the base.

### Leaves

Using the dark green ribbon, work the leaves with a mix of ribbon and straight stitch, adding a few twists to some of the stitches. Add some light green leaves close to the stems.

### Embroidery key

*All thread embroidery is worked with one strand.*

#### Flowers and buds

Petals = B (detached chain)
Calyx = C (straight stitch)
Petal markings = A (French knot, 2–3 wraps)

Stems = A (stem stitch)

Leaves = C or D (ribbon stitch, folded ribbon stitch, straight stitch)

# CROWN IMPERIAL

## by Angela Dower

### This design uses

*Back stitch, Couching, Folded ribbon stitch,
Granitos, Long and short stitch, Loop stitch,
Raised stem stitch, Ribbon stitch, Straight
stitch, Whipping*

#### Ribbon embroidery index
Couching 11
Folded ribbon stitch 24
Loop stitch 19
Ribbon stitch 23

## Materials

### Threads & ribbons

*DMC stranded cotton*
A = 745 vy lt yellow
*Needle Necessities overdyed floss*
B = 130 woodland fantasy
*Rajmahal Art silk*
C = 104 cinnamon
*YLI silk floss*
D = 157 drab olive
*Colour Streams hand dyed silk ribbon 4mm
(³⁄₁₆") wide*
E = 1m (39 ½") no. 32 berry
F = 2m (2yd 7") no. 26 Tuscan olive
*Colour Streams hand dyed silk ribbon 7mm
(⁵⁄₁₆") wide*
G = 2m (2yd 7") no. 32 berry

### Needles

No. 5 straw (milliner's) needle
No. 9 straw (milliner's) needle
No. 20 chenille needle
No. 26 tapestry needle

### Supplies

Dressmaker's awl

## Order of work

Use the chenille needle for all ribbon
embroidery. The no. 9 straw needle is used
when working with one strand of thread
and the no. 5 straw needle when working
with several strands of thread. Use the
tapestry needle for the raised stem stitch.

### Main stem

Outline each side of the main stem in
back stitch. Pad the centre of the stem
by stitching two rows of long and short
stitch. Add evenly spaced horizontal
straight stitches along the length of the
stem to form the framework for the
raised stem stitch. Densely fill the stem
with rows of raised stem stitch.

## Flower heads

Embroider each flower separately,
working them in the order shown on
the diagram (*diag 1*). Use the darker
sections of the ribbon for the back petals
and the lighter parts for the front petals.
As the ribbon passes through the same
hole in the fabric several times, enlarge
the hole with the awl.

Using the wide
ribbon, work a
1cm (³⁄₈") loop
stitch for the first
flower. Fold the
loop down and
couch the two
lower corners with
thread. Add a
ribbon stitch petal
over the loop
stitch with the
narrow ribbon
(*diag 2*).

*Diag 1*

*Diag 2*

For the remaining flowers, work the
back petal in ribbon stitch using the
narrow ribbon. Embroider the side
petals in folded ribbon stitch using the
wide ribbon. Ensure that the ribbon
folds in half with the fold towards the
side of the flower as you pull the ribbon
through. Secure the under layer of the
petal with a tiny back stitch if necessary.

Embroider the stamens before
working the centre petal of each flower.
Work a granitos of four to six straight
stitches for the end of each stamen. Link
this to the petals with a long straight
stitch. Using the cinnamon thread, add a
straight stitch along the left hand side of
each granitos to create a shaded effect.

The central petal of each flower is a
folded ribbon stitch, which is then
manipulated. First, work a folded ribbon
stitch. After completing the stitch, gently
lift it and turn the tip over so the curl on

the side of the ribbon faces the fabric. Fine tweezers can be an aid in turning the ribbon. Gently pull the ribbon until the stitch settles back on the fabric (diags 3A & 3B).

Diag 3A    Diag 3B

## Small stems

Bring five strands of thread to the front of the fabric at the top of one flower. Remove four strands from the needle. Using the remaining thread, whip around the other four until the stem is the desired length. Take the whipping thread through the last wrap to secure it. Rethread the four strands into the needle. Take them to the back at the top of the main stem and end off. Repeat for the remaining small stems.

## Leaves

Work each leaf loosely at first as you can tighten them later by pulling from the insertion point on the back before securing. Work the leaves in folded ribbon stitch and ribbon stitch, couching the folds of the folded ribbon stitches if necessary.

## Embroidery key

*All thread embroidery is worked with one strand unless otherwise specified.*

### Main stem

Outline = B (back stitch)
Padding = B (3 strands, long and short stitch)
Surface = B (raised stem stitch)

### First flower

Petals = G (loop stitch, couching), E (ribbon stitch), C (couching)

### Remaining flowers

Back petal = E (ribbon stitch)
Side petals = G (folded ribbon stitch), C (couching)
Central petal = G (folded ribbon stitch)
Stamens = A (granitos, straight stitch), C (straight stitch)

*Small stems* = B (5 strands, whipping)

*Leaves* = F (folded ribbon stitch), D (couching)

# BUFF BEAUTY

## by Carolyn Pearce

### This design uses

*Beading, Colonial knot, Detached chain,
Fly stitch, Running stitch – colonial knot
combination, Ribbon stitch, Spider web rose,
Stem stitch, Straight stitch,
Twirled ribbon rose*

### Ribbon embroidery index

Colonial knot 9
Ribbon stitch 23
Running stitch – colonial knot
combination 28
Spider web rose 30
Stem stitch 31
Stem stitch rose 99
Twirled ribbon rose 36

## Materials

### Threads, ribbon & beads

*Au Ver à Soie, Soie d'Alger*
A = F1 cream
*Rajmahal Art silk*
B = ecru
*Anchor Marlitt stranded rayon*
C = 1036 lt beige
*Kacoonda hand dyed silk ribbon 4mm
(³/₁₆") wide*
D = 2m (2yd 7") no. 4 cream
*Mill Hill petite glass beads*
E = 40123 cream

### Needles

No. 8 crewel needle
No. 10 crewel needle
No. 12 crewel needle
No. 22 chenille needle

### Supplies

White beading thread (eg *Nymo*)

## Order of work

Use the no. 22 chenille needle when working with the silk ribbon, the no. 10 crewel needle for the silk thread, the no. 8 crewel needle for the rayon thread and the no. 12 needle for the art silk thread and beading.

### Large central rose

Work eight colonial knots in a tight cluster for the centre. Surround the centre with two rows of stem stitch, placed close together, for the petals.

### Medium roses

Work four spider web roses around the large rose. After each rose is completed, attach a tiny bead in the centre.

### Small roses

Stitch four twirled ribbon roses between the spider web roses and a running stitch – colonial knot combination rose at each end of the central design.

### Rosebuds

Three rosebuds are embroidered at each end of the design. Work each rosebud with two ribbon stitches for the petals, making one slightly longer than the other. For the calyx, surround each bud with a fly stitch, then work a straight stitch over the top of the petals.

### Forget-me-nots

Stitch each forget-me-not with a tiny bead for the centre and five colonial knots for the petals.

### Tiny buds

Work groups of three colonial knots among the ribbon rosebuds.

### Leaves and twigs

Embroider pairs of tiny detached chain leaves along each end of the spray, then pairs or groups of three around the central design. Using fly stitch, work pairs of twigs around the centre spray, finishing each one with a long anchoring stitch.

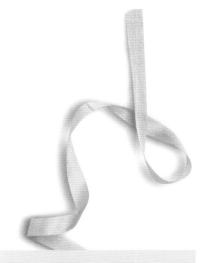

## Embroidery key

*All thread embroidery is worked with one strand unless otherwise specified.*

### Large central rose

Centre = D (colonial knot)
Petals = D (stem stitch)

### Medium roses

Framework = C (straight stitch)
Petals = D (spider web rose)
Centre = E (beading)

### Small roses

Petals = D (twirled ribbon rose, running stitch – colonial knot combination)

### Rosebuds

Petals = D (ribbon stitch)
Calyx = B (fly stitch, straight stitch)

### Forget-me-nots

Centre = E (beading)
Petals = C (colonial knot)

### Tiny buds = A (2 strands, colonial knot)

### Leaves and twigs

Leaves = B (detached chain)
Twigs = B (fly stitch)

# STEM STITCH ROSE

↑ indicates top of fabric

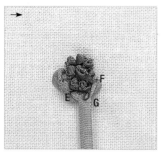

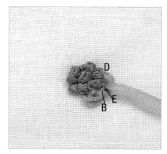

**1 Centre.** Work eight colonial knots in a tight cluster for the centre.

**2 Inner petals.** Bring the ribbon to the front at A. Take the needle to the back at B and re-emerge at C, keeping the ribbon below the needle.

**3** Pull the ribbon through to complete the first stem stitch.

**4** Take the needle to the back at D and re-emerge at E, close to B and pull through.

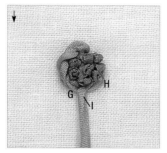

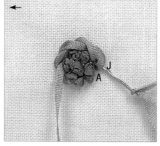

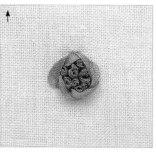

**5** Rotate the fabric. Work a third stitch from E to F. Re-emerge at G.

**6** Rotate the fabric. Work a fourth stitch from G to H, re-emerging at I.

**7** Rotate the fabric. Take the needle to the back at J, just beyond A and on the outside of the first stitch.

**8** Pull the thread through.

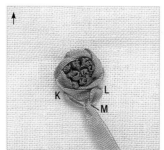

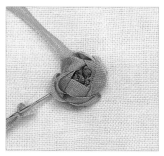

**9 Outer petals.** Bring the needle to the front at K, halfway along and on the outside of the first stitch.

**10** Pull the thread through. Rotate the fabric. Work a stitch from K to L, emerging at M.

**11** Work four more stitches with the last stitch over-lapping the first stitch of this round. Rotate the fabric as you work.

**12** Pull the ribbon through and end off on the back of the fabric. **Completed stem stitch rose.**

# BOUQUET OF ROSES

## by Carolyn Pearce

### This design uses

*Bullion knot, Colonial knot, Couching, Detached chain, Feather stitch, Fly stitch, French knot, Running stitch – colonial knot combination, Split stitch, Stem stitch, Straight stitch, Tied bow*

### Ribbon embroidery index

Couching 11
Running stitch – colonial knot combination 28

## Materials

### Threads & ribbons

*Au Ver à Soie, Soie d'Alger*
A = 1712 lt Williamsburg blue
B = 3423 med silver-green
C = 4140 ice blue
D = 4621 vy lt dusty mauve
E = F19 chicken soup
*Au Ver à Soie, antique metallic thread*
F = 222 gold
*YLI 601 fine metallic thread*
G = 7 iced green
*YLI silk ribbon 2mm (⅛") wide*
H = 40cm (16") no. 90 vy lt antique blue
*Colour Streams hand dyed silk ribbon 4mm (³⁄₁₆") wide*
I = 1m (39 ½") rose blush

### Needles

No. 10 straw (milliner's) needle
No. 12 crewel needle
No. 22 chenille needle

### Supplies

Lace pins

## Order of work

Use the chenille needle for the ribbon embroidery, the straw needle for the bullion knots and the crewel needle for all other embroidery.

### Bow

Tie the blue ribbon into a small bow with long tails. Fold the tails to form delicate twists and hold in place with lace pins. Couch the bow and tails with colonial knots.

### Roses and leaves

Stitch six running stitch – colonial knot combination roses. Work a central rose first, then the remaining five roses in a circle around it.

Using the iced green metallic thread, embroider nine large fly stitch leaves around the outer edge of the roses.

### Forget-me-nots

Scatter tiny blue forget-me-nots around the large leaves and the roses. Each forget-me-not is worked with five blue colonial knots for the petals and a gold colonial knot for the centre.

Add tiny sprays of four buds. For each spray, work a pair of colonial knots at the base and a single colonial knot above. Stitch a French knot at the tip.

### Rosebuds

Embroider five pairs of bullion knot buds around the outer edge of the bouquet. Use two bullion knots, worked side by side, for the petals. Surround each bud with a fly stitch that has a long anchoring stitch. Work two tiny straight stitches at the tip. Stitch two tiny detached chain leaves near each pair of rosebuds.

### Stems and twigs

Stitch three long stems in stem stitch below the bow knot. Work the four remaining stems in split stitch.

Using the gold thread, fill any spaces around the outer edge of the design with feather stitch twigs.

## Embroidery Key

*All thread embroidery is worked with one strand.*

*Bow* = H (tied ribbon), C (colonial knot)

*Roses* = I (running stitch – colonial knot combination)

Leaves = G (fly stitch)

### Forget-me-nots

Flower petals = A (colonial knot)
Centre = E (colonial knot)
Buds = A (colonial knot, French knot, 1 wrap)

### Rosebuds

Petals = D (2 bullion knots, 8 wraps)
Calyx = B (fly stitch, straight stitch)
Leaves = F (detached chain)

### Stems and twigs

Stems = B (split stitch), G (stem stitch)
Twigs = F (feather stitch)

# ROSES IN MINIATURE

## by Shirley Sinclair

### This design uses

*Couching, Colonial knot, Fly stitch, Folded toothpick rose, Ribbon stitch, Stem stitch, Straight stitch, Tied bow*

### Materials

#### Threads & ribbons

*Madeira stranded cotton*
A = 1503 avocado green
B = 2210 dk old gold
*Kacoonda hand dyed silk ribbon 4mm (³⁄₁₆") wide*
C = 2m (2yd 7") no. 101 sunset rose
*YLI silk ribbon 2mm (⅛") wide*
D = 50cm (20") no. 20 med forest green
E = 15cm (6") no. 56 med olive green

#### Needles

No. 8 crewel needle
No. 12 between needle
No. 22 chenille needle

#### Supplies

Matching quilting thread
Toothpick

### Order of work

Use the between needle for securing the toothpick roses, the chenille needle for working with the ribbon and the crewel needle for all remaining thread embroidery.

#### Roses

Make seven folded toothpick roses. Attach each one to the background fabric with two or three tiny back stitches using the quilting thread.

## Buds and stems

Embroider the buds in ribbon stitch. Work the stems for the buds followed by the main posy stems. For each calyx work a fly stitch with a straight stitch in between. Embroider a pair of straight stitches at the tip of each bud.

## Leaves

Using ribbon stitch, work the leaves along the bud stems and the stem at the top. Embroider a few more leaves around the roses, tucking the ends of some of them under the roses.

## Sprays

Using the old gold thread, embroider the small sprays of flowers. Work two to four colonial knots for each spray.

## Bow

Tie a bow, with small loops and long tails, in the olive green ribbon. Attach the bow below the roses with two to three tiny stitches.

Take the tails of ribbon to the back of the fabric, forming a fold in each tail. Catch the edge of the folds with a tiny couching stitch using the quilting thread.

## Embroidery key

*All thread embroidery is worked with one strand.*

Roses = C (folded toothpick rose)

### Buds

Petal = C (ribbon stitch)
Calyx = A (fly stitch, straight stitch)
Tip = A (straight stitch)

Stems = A (stem stitch)

Leaves = D (ribbon stitch)

Sprays = B (colonial knot)

### Bow

Loops = E (tied bow)
Tails = E (couching)

# FOLDED TOOTHPICK ROSE

1 Moisten one end of ribbon. Lay toothpick on moistened ribbon with tip approx half way across width of ribbon.

2 Fold over end of ribbon for approx 10mm (⅜") and wrap ribbon around toothpick 2–3 times to secure.

3 With the left hand, fold the upper edge of the ribbon back and down.

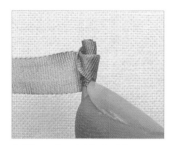

4 Wrap the folded ribbon once around the centre to form a petal.

5 Continue folding the ribbon back and rolling it tightly around the toothpick 5–6 times.

6 Trim the ribbon, leaving a 6mm (¼") tail. Pinch the base of the rose. Slowly remove the rose from the toothpick.

7 Using thread, secure the tail and base of the rose with 3–4 tiny back stitches.

8 Trim the tail of ribbon close to the stitching. **Completed folded toothpick rose.**

# GRAPE HYACINTHS

## by Helen Eriksson

### This design uses

*Folded ribbon stitch, French knot, Ribbon stitch, Straight stitch*

### Ribbon embroidery index

Folded ribbon stitch 24
French knot 16
Ribbon stitch 23
Straight stitch 33

## Materials

### Thread & ribbons

Anchor stranded cotton
A = 269 ultra dk avocado green
*YLI silk ribbon 4mm (³/₁₆") wide*
B = 1.5m (1yd 23") no. 20 forest green
C = 50cm (20") no. 22 lavender
D = 1m (39 ½") no. 117 hyacinth
E = 1m (39 ½") no. 18 dk hyacinth
*Kacoonda hand dyed silk ribbon 4mm (³/₁₆") wide*
F = 40cm (16") no. 3B dk blue-violet

### Needles

No. 8 crewel needle
No. 20 chenille needle

## Order of work

Use the chenille needle for the ribbon embroidery and the crewel needle for all thread embroidery.

### Flowers

Randomly stitch French knots in a triangular shape using D, E and F. Place the knots close together. Add some lavender knots, varying the numbers used in each triangle.

### Stems and leaves

Embroider the stems with straight stitches. Add the leaves using straight stitches, loose ribbon stitches and folded ribbon stitches.

### Embroidery key

*All thread embroidery is worked with two strands.*

*Flowers* = C, D, E and F (French knot, 1 wrap)

*Stems* = A (straight stitch)

*Leaves* = B (straight stitch, ribbon stitch, folded ribbon stitch), A (straight stitch)

*Golden Threads*

103

# ROSES AND FORGET-ME-NOTS

## by Carolyn Pearce

### This design uses

*Beading, Colonial knot, Detached chain,
Fly stitch, Ribbon stitch, Smocker's knot,
Straight stitch, Twisted detached chain,
Whipped straight stitch*

### Ribbon embroidery index

Ribbon rosebud 24
Ribbon stitch 23
Twisted detached chain 13
Whipped straight stitch 35
Whipped straight stitch rose 105

## Materials

### Threads, ribbons & beads

DMC stranded cotton
A = 642 dk beige-grey
*Au Ver à Soie, Soie d'Alger*
B = 4140 ice blue
C = 4222 lt golden chestnut
*Rajmahal Art silk*
D = 421 green earth
*YLI 601 fine metallic thread*
E = 7 iced green
*YLI silk ribbon 4mm (³⁄₁₆") wide*

F = 1m (39 ½") no. 158 dk dusky pink
*Vintage Ribbons hand dyed silk ribbon
4mm (³⁄₁₆") wide*
G = 50cm (20") peaches and cream
H = 60cm (24") blush
I = 1m (39 ½") pine needles
*Maria George size 9 beads*
J = 907 cream
*Mill Hill glass seed beads*
K = 00123 cream
L = 00557 gold
*Mill Hill antique glass beads*
M = 03051 misty
*Mill Hill petite glass beads*
N = 40123 cream

### Needles

No. 10 crewel needle
No. 22 chenille needle

### Supplies

White beading thread (eg *Nymo*)

## Order of work

Use the chenille needle for the ribbon
embroidery and the crewel needle for all
other embroidery.

### Rose, rosebuds and leaves

Stitch the large rose following the step-
by-step instructions. Stitch the rosebuds
and leaves next. Each leaf is a twisted
detached chain with a straight stitch at
the tip and a smocker's knot at the base.

### Pink forget-me-nots

For each flower, place six pink beads
onto the thread. Take the thread through
the first three beads again and pull
firmly to form a small circle. Place a gold
bead onto the thread and take the
needle back through the sixth bead. Tie
the two ends of the thread in a tight
knot and use the tails to couch the
beads to the fabric.

### White sprays

Work each spray with two large beads,
two or three seed beads and three or
four petite beads.

### Blue forget-me-nots

Scatter tiny forget-me-nots around the
edge of the design. Add pairs of
detached chain leaves near some
of them.

### Embroidery key

*All thread embroidery is worked with
one strand unless otherwise specified.*

#### Whipped rose

Centre = F (colonial knot)
Inner petals = G (whipped
straight stitch)
Outer petals = G and H (whipped
straight stitch)

#### Rosebuds

Centre = F (twisted detached chain)
Petals = G (ribbon stitch)
Calyx = I (ribbon stitch), A (fly stitch,
straight stitch, smocker's knot)
Highlights = E (fly stitch,
straight stitch)
Leaves = I (twisted detached
chain), A (straight stitch,
smocker's knot)

#### Pink forget-me-nots

Petals = M (beading)
Centre = L (beading)

*White sprays* = J, K and N (beading)

#### Blue forget-me-nots

Centre = C (2 strands, colonial knot)
Petals = B (2 strands, colonial knot)
Leaves = D (detached chain)

# WHIPPED STRAIGHT STITCH ROSE

1 **Centre.** Using the darkest shade of ribbon, work three colonial knots close together.

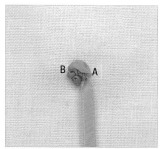

2 **Inner petals.** Change ribbon. Work a straight stitch from A to B.

3 Bring the ribbon to the front just below and to the left of A.

4 Take the needle over the straight stitch and then under it. The needle does not go through the fabric.

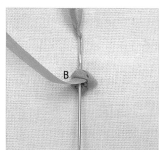

5 Again, take the needle under the straight stitch, positioning it near B.

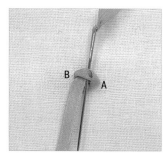

6 Pull through to form a second wrap. Take the needle under the straight stitch halfway between A and B.

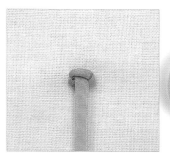

7 Pull the ribbon through. Work another wrap over the middle wrap in the same manner as before.

8 Take the ribbon to the back of the fabric behind the whipped stitch.

9 Pull the ribbon through. Work a second whipped straight stitch in the same manner, below the centre.

10 **Outer petals.** Using G for one stitch and H for the others, work three whipped straight stitches. Increase the number of wraps by two.

11 Work three more whipped straight stitches using H. Increase the number of wraps by two. **Completed whipped straight stitch rose.**

# ROSE BOUQUET

## by Beverley Gogel

### This design uses

*Bullion knot, Colonial knot, Detached chain,*
*French knot, Folded ribbon rose, Grab stitch,*
*Loop stitch, Looped straight stitch,*
*Padded straight stitch Ribbon filler,*
*Ribbon stitch, Straight stitch*

### Materials

*Threads & ribbons*

Pale pink machine sewing thread
*DMC stranded cotton*
A = 225 ultra lt shell pink
B = 819 lt baby pink
C = 3012 med khaki green
D = 3013 lt khaki green
*YLI silk ribbon 4mm (³⁄₁₆") wide*
E = 1m (39 ½") no. 56 olive green
*YLI silk ribbon 7mm (⁵⁄₁₆") wide*
F = 2m (2yd 7") no. 157 dusky pink

*Needles*

No. 1 straw (milliner's) needle
No. 5 straw (milliner's) needle
No. 22 chenille needle

### Order of work

Use the no. 22 chenille needle for the
ribbon and the no. 1 straw needle for
the bullion knots. The no. 5 straw needle
is used for all remaining
thread embroidery.

*Bow*

Stitch four loop stitches for the bow
loops and two looped straight stitches
for the ties. Form the bow knot with a
padded straight stitch.

*Roses*

Make four folded ribbon roses and stitch
them in a cluster above the bow.

### Ribbon fillers

Cut two pieces of F, each 10cm (4") long. Fashion each piece into a ribbon filler with three loops. Attach one filler at each side of the roses.

### Large buds

Using ribbon, embroider three pink buds with straight stitches.

### Bullion buds

Embroider two pairs of bullion knot buds, placing one pair at the top and one on the left hand side of the bouquet.

### Colonial knot buds

Stitch a single ribbon bud on each side of the roses and one at the top. Stitch two pairs of ribbon buds above the roses. Each pair of buds is worked with a loose colonial knot for the lower one. Work a tighter colonial knot for the bud on the upper right hand side and stitch a colonial knot in thread for the upper bud on the left hand side.

### Small buds

Work these buds with one straight stitch, using six strands of thread doubled in the needle.

### Foliage

Using ribbon, stitch the detached chain leaves in a semi-circle around the outer edge of the roses. Work two looped stitches among the roses.

Add the calyxes to all the buds with a grab stitch around the base and a straight stitch along one side, using blended threads. Complete the ribbon leaves with the same grab stitch, straight stitch combination. Scatter straight stitches and French knots around the outer edge.

## Embroidery key

*All thread embroidery is worked with two strands unless otherwise specified.*

### Bow

Loops = F (loop stitch)
Ties = F (looped straight stitch)
Knot = F (padded straight stitch)

*Roses* = F (folded ribbon rose)

*Ribbon fillers* = F

### Large buds

Petals = F (straight stitch)
Calyx = C blended with D (1 strand of each, straight stitch, grab stitch)

### Bullion buds

Petals = A (6 strands, 1 bullion knot, 12–14 wraps)
Calyx = C blended with D (1 strand of each, straight stitch, grab stitch)

### Colonial knot buds

Petals = F (colonial knot), B (12 strands, colonial knot)

### Small buds

Petals = B (straight stitch)
Calyx = C blended with D (1 strand of each, straight stitch, grab stitch)

### Foliage

Ribbon leaves = E (detached chain), C blended with D (1 strand of each, straight stitch, grab stitch)
Scattered foliage = C blended with D (1 strand of each, straight stitch, French knot, 1–2 wraps)
Ribbon loops = E (loop stitch)

*Constant Friends*

# POSY OF FLOWERS

by Helen Eriksson

## This design uses

*Beading, Couching, Loop stitch, Feather stitch, Fly stitch, Folded ribbon rose, French knot, Grab stitch, Ribbon stitch, Stem stitch, Straight stitch, Tied bow, Twisted straight stitch*

### Ribbon embroidery index

Couching 11
Folded ribbon rose 14
French knot 16
Grab stitch 19
Loop stitch 19
Ribbon stitch 23
Straight stitch 33
Twisted straight stitch 34

## Materials

### Threads, ribbons & beads

Matching machine sewing thread for folded roses and gold cord
*Anchor stranded cotton*
A = 846 vy dk khaki green
*YLI no. 601 fine metallic thread*
B = gold
*Hand dyed double sided satin ribbon 15mm (⅝") wide*
C = 80cm (31 ½") dusky pink
D = 60cm (24") vy lt antique mauve
E = 60cm (24") mocha
*Hand dyed double sided satin ribbon 7mm (⁵⁄₁₆") wide*
F = 1m (39 ½") dusky pink
G = 80cm (31 ½") vy lt antique mauve
*Hanah hand dyed bias cut silk ribbon 11mm (⁷⁄₁₆") wide*
H = 60cm (24") olde English Xmas
*Kacoonda hand dyed silk ribbon 4mm (³⁄₁₆") wide*
I = 3m (3yd 10") no. 308 winter mist
*Mokuba no. 4882 gradation rayon ribbon 12mm (½") wide*
J = 1m (39 ½") no. 1 marshland
*Mokuba no. 4546 crepe georgette ribbon 9mm (⅜") wide*
K = 90cm (35 ½") no. 49 coffee
*Mokuba no. 1505 rayon ribbon 8mm (⁵⁄₁₆") wide*
L = 1.8m (1yd 35") no. 16 dk green
*Mokuba no. 1542 azlon tape 3.5mm (⅛") wide*
M = 2m (2yd 7") no. 16 olive green
*YLI silk ribbon 4mm (³⁄₁₆") wide*
N = 80cm (31 ½") no. 21 dk forest green
O = 30cm (12") no. 54 old gold
P = 2m (2yd 7") no. 72 dk olive green
Q = 1.5m (1yd 23") no. 179 dk antique violet
*Maria George Delica beads*
R = DBR 22 metallic bronze
S = 40cm (16") gold cord

### Needles

No. 9 sharp needle
No. 16 chenille needle
No. 22 chenille needle

## Order of work

Use the photograph as a guide for colour changes within the design.

Use the no. 16 chenille needle for the 7mm and 8mm (⁵⁄₁₆"), 9mm (⅜") and 12mm (½") ribbons. The no. 22 chenille needle is used for the azlon tape and the 4mm (³⁄₁₆") ribbons. The sharp needle is used for the beading and all thread embroidery.

### Large posy

#### Main stems

Embroider the main stems for the posy, using L, N and P. Work each stem with a twisted straight stitch.

#### Large roses and leaves

Work ten large folded ribbon roses. Each rose is formed from a 20cm (8") length of ribbon. Attach the roses to the fabric keeping them in a cluster.

Fill any gaps between the roses with loop stitch and work ribbon stitch leaves around the outer edge of the roses.

#### Rosebuds

Embroider the rosebuds around the cluster of roses. Work the petals for each bud with either a pair of ribbon stitches overlapping them at the base, or a single ribbon stitch.

Work a straight stitch on each side of some of the petals and one to three over the petals for the calyx. On some of the buds work a long anchoring stitch for the stem, twisting it until it becomes thin. For the remaining buds embroider a grab stitch or fly stitch at the base with a long anchoring stitch twisted tightly for the stems.

Work two to five straight stitches at the tip of some of the buds.

#### Lilac

Embroider the stems in stem stitch, using the stranded cotton.

Work clusters of tightly packed French knots using I and Q for the flowers. Mingle the two colours within each flower head.

### Fern fronds

Stitch the six fern fronds next. Begin each one with a single ribbon stitch at the tip. Alternating from side to side, work pairs of ribbon stitches from the centre outwards. Work the stems in stem stitch.

### Gold twigs

Work each sprig in feather stitch, adding a few small straight stitches. Work additional gold straight stitches among the buds and leaves.

### Blossoms

Stitch five blossoms in the coffee georgette ribbon. Work five ribbon stitch petals for each one. Highlight each petal with four to six straight stitches, radiating them from the centre. For the centre, work a French knot and surround it with seven or eight tiny bronze beads.

### Bow

Using the gold cord, bring the tails to the front on each side of the stems. Tie the cord into a loose bow. Form a knot at the end of each tail and couch in place. Trim any excess cord. Stitch the loops, knot and ties in place using matching machine sewing thread.

## Small rose spray

### Rose

Work a small folded ribbon rose, in the same manner as the large roses, using a 10cm (4") length of ribbon. Attach the rose to the fabric.

Stitch the calyx with a straight stitch and two tiny loop stitches at the base of the rose using L. Change to N and work a small straight stitch and a grab stitch with a long anchoring stitch, twisting it tightly. Couch the centre of the stem forming a curve.

### Rosebuds

Embroider two rosebuds, each with a single ribbon stitch petal. Work the calyxes with straight stitches.

Change to N and work a grab stitch with a long anchoring stitch, twisting it tightly for the stems. Stitch three or four straight stitches at the tip of each bud.

### Lilac, gold twigs and leaves

Work these in the same manner as the large posy. Add three ribbon stitch leaves and link each one to the nearest stem with a grab stitch.

## Embroidery key

*All thread embroidery is worked with one strand.*

### Large posy

*Large roses* = C, D or E (folded ribbon rose)

**Rosebuds**
Petals = F or G (ribbon stitch)
Calyx = L, N or P (ribbon stitch, straight stitch)
Tip = A (straight stitch) or none
Stems = L, N or P (grab stitch, fly stitch)

**Lilac**
Flowers = I and Q (French knot, 1 wrap)
Stems = A (stem stitch)

**Blossoms**
Petals = K (ribbon stitch)
Petal highlights = B (straight stitch)
Centre = O (French knot, 1 wrap), R (beading)

**Leaves and stems**
Main stems = L, N or P (twisted straight stitch)
Leaves = H or J (loop stitch, ribbon stitch)
Fern fronds = A (stem stitch), M (ribbon stitch)
Gold twigs = B (feather stitch, straight stitch)
*Bow* = S (tied bow), machine sewing thread (couching)

## Blossom spray

Work the blossom, lilac and fern fronds in the same manner as the large posy. Finally, add four branches of gold twigs and the ribbon stitch leaf.

### Rose spray

**Rose**
Petals = F (folded ribbon rose)
Calyx = L (loop stitch, straight stitch)
Stem = N (straight stitch, grab stitch, couching)

**Rosebuds**
Petals = F (ribbon stitch)
Calyx = L (straight stitch)
Stem = N (grab stitch)
Tip = A (straight stitch)

**Lilac**
Flowers = I and Q (French knot, 1 wrap)
Stems = A (stem stitch)
*Leaves* = J or L (ribbon stitch), A (grab stitch)
*Gold twigs* = B (feather stitch, straight stitch)

### Blossom spray

**Blossom**
Petals = K (ribbon stitch)
Centre = O (French knot, 1 wrap), R (beading)
Leaf = J (ribbon stitch), A (grab stitch)

**Lilac**
Flowers = I and Q (French knot, 1 wrap)
Stems = A (stem stitch)
*Fern fronds* = A (stem stitch), M (ribbon stitch)
*Gold twigs* = B (feather stitch, straight stitch)

# BABY BEARS

## by Kari Mecca

### This design uses
*Couching, Detached chain, Fly stitch, French knot, Loop stitch, Satin stitch, Straight stitch*

### Ribbon embroidery index
Couching 11
Detached chain 12
Fly stitch 13
Loop stitch 19
Loop stitch bow 20
Straight stitch 33

## Materials

### Thread & ribbons
*DMC stranded cotton*
A = 310 black
*YLI silk ribbon 7mm (⁵⁄₁₆") wide*
B = 50cm (20") no. 3 white
C = 50cm (20") no. 5 blush pink
D = 50cm (20") no. 125 powder blue
*YLI silk ribbon 4mm (³⁄₁₆") wide*
E = 50cm (20") no. 8 med soft pink
F = 50cm (20") no. 9 baby blue
G = 50cm (20") no. 31 lt pistachio green

### Needles
No. 8 crewel needle
No. 18 chenille needle
No. 22 chenille needle

## Order of work
Use the no. 18 chenille needle for the 7mm (⁵⁄₁₆") ribbons and the no. 22 chenille needle for the 4mm (³⁄₁₆") ribbons. The crewel needle is used for all thread embroidery.

### Bears
Both bears are stitched in the same manner.

Beginning at the neck, stitch a large detached chain for the head. Embroider a straight stitch for each ear, taking the ribbon to the back of the fabric behind the head. Stitch a straight stitch from the centre of the head to the neck for the muzzle.

Work a triangle of horizontal satin stitches for the nose and a vertical straight stitch for the mouth. Add the French knot eyes at the upper edge of the muzzle.

Stitch a loose detached chain for each bow loop. Work straight stitches for the bow knot and ties.

### Dummy
Embroider a straight stitch for the teat. Twist the green ribbon and stitch a detached chain for the handle. Finish with a straight stitch across the base of the teat.

### Rattle
Stitch a detached chain for the ball. Twist the green ribbon and work a straight stitch across the detached chain. Using the same ribbon, couch the straight stitch at the centre. Keeping the ribbon twisted, embroider an uneven fly stitch for the handle.

Work two straight stitches for the ties of the bow. Stitch a loop stitch bow using a 10mm (³⁄₈") loop.

### Bottle
Embroider two straight stitches side by side for the bottle. Work a straight stitch for the top of the teat. Complete the teat with two straight stitches across the top of the bottle. Add three very short straight stitches over the ribbon on one side of the bottle for measurement markings.

## Embroidery key
*All thread embroidery is worked with one strand.*

### Bears
Head = C or D (detached chain)
Ears = C or D (straight stitch)
Muzzle = B (straight stitch)
Eyes = A (French knot, 2 wraps)
Nose = A (satin stitch)
Mouth = A (straight stitch)
Bow loops = E or F (detached chain)
Bow knot and ties = E or F (straight stitch)

### Dummy
Teat = C (straight stitch)
Handle = G (detached chain, straight stitch)

### Rattle
Ball = E (detached chain), G (straight stitch, couching)
Handle = G (fly stitch)
Bow = F (loop stitch, straight stitch)

### Bottle
Bottle = C (straight stitch)
Teat = G (straight stitch)
Measurement markings = A (straight stitch)

# BEARS IN THE GARDEN

## by Jenny Saladine

## This design uses

*Fly stitch, French knot, Long and short stitch, Ribbon stitch, Satin stitch, Stem stitch, Straight stitch*

### Ribbon embroidery index

French knot 16
Ribbon stitch 23
Stem stitch 31
Straight stitch 33

## Materials

### Threads & ribbons

*DMC stranded cotton*
A = 524 vy lt fern green
B = 3031 brown groundings
C = 3052 med green-grey
D = 3371 black-brown
*Au Ver à Soie, Soie d'Alger*
E = F20 egg shell
F = 4533 med mocha
G = 4535 dk mocha
*YLI silk ribbon 2mm (⅛") wide*

H = 2m (2yd 7") no. 5 blush pink
I = 20cm (8") no. 15 bright yellow
J = 50cm (20") no. 156 cream
*YLI silk ribbon 4mm (³⁄₁₆") wide*
K = 50cm (20") no. 101 blue-violet
L = 1m (39 ½") no. 155 pale lichen green
*Kacoonda hand dyed silk ribbon 4mm (³⁄₁₆") wide*
M = 1m (39 ½") no. 3C hydrangea
N = 1m (39 ½") no. 304 dusky blue
O = 1m (39 ½") no. 305 dk dusky blue
P = 1m (39 ½") no. 306 autumn green
Q = 1m (39 ½") no. 307 winter green
*Colour Streams hand dyed silk ribbon 4mm (³⁄₁₆") wide*
R = 50cm (20") dusky mauve
S = 50cm (20") antique rose
T = 20cm (8") wisteria
*Bucilla silk ribbon 7mm (⁵⁄₁₆") wide*
U = 1m (39 ½") no. 27-024 lavender
V = 1.5m (1yd 23") no. 24-633 pale hunter

### Needles

No. 9 crewel needle
No. 22 chenille needle

## Order of work

Use the photograph as a guide for colour changes within the design.

Use the chenille needle for the silk ribbons and the crewel needle for all thread embroidery.

### Bears

Embroider each eye with two tiny horizontal straight stitches then work two vertical straight stitches over the top. Work the nose in satin stitch with a vertical straight stitch below to divide the muzzle. Stitch the head, then the outer section of the ears with long and short stitch and satin stitch. Fill the inner section of the ears with straight stitch or long and short stitch and then work the muzzle.

Embroider the partial body of the bear in the lower right hand corner with long and short stitch.

### Roses and rosebuds

Work one or two rounds of stem stitch for the petals of the pink and cream roses. Stitch a straight stitch in the centre of each rose.

Embroider the petals of the rosebuds with overlapping straight stitches. To work the calyx, surround each flower with a fly stitch and a straight stitch over the base of the petals. Embroider the stems for the buds in straight stitch.

Stitch the leaves of the roses and buds in straight stitch and ribbon stitch.

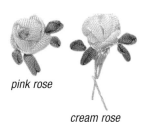

*pink rose*

*cream rose*

## Wisteria

Embroider each raceme with clusters of French knots. Work loose French knots in the lighter shade of ribbon and tight French knots in the darker shade.

Embroider the leaves in straight stitch or ribbon stitch, tucking some of them in among the flowers.

*wisteria*

## Delphiniums

Starting at the base of each flower, work the petals in straight stitch. Fill in around the petals with ribbon stitch leaves and straight stitches using the stranded cotton.

*delphinium*

## Hydrangeas

Work the hydrangea flowers on the lower left with clusters of tightly packed French knots. Add pairs of ribbon stitch leaves around the flowers.

*hydrangeas*

## Lavender

Work the lavender in the upper half of the design. Stitch the flowers in straight stitch and the leaves in ribbon stitch. Add straight stitches for the stems.

*lavender*

## Grass

Using long straight stitches, work the grass in the lower section of the design. Randomly fill any remaining spaces with long straight stitches, using the stranded cotton.

*grass*

## Embroidery key

*All thread embroidery is worked with one strand.*

### Bears

Eyes = D (straight stitch)
Nose = D (satin stitch)
Line under nose = D (straight stitch) or none
Head = F or G (long and short stitch)
Outer ear = F or G (long and short stitch, satin stitch)
Inner ear = B or G (satin stitch, straight stitch)
Muzzle = E (long and short stitch, satin stitch)
Partial body on lower right bear = F (long and short stitch)

### Pink roses and rosebuds

Rose centre = H or S (straight stitch)
Rose petals = H (stem stitch)
Bud petal = H or S (straight stitch)
Bud calyx = A or C (fly stitch, straight stitch)
Stems = A (straight stitch)
Leaves = Q (ribbon stitch)

### Cream roses and rosebuds

Rose centre = I or J (straight stitch)
Rose petals = J (stem stitch)
Bud petal = J (straight stitch)
Bud calyx = A (fly stitch, straight stitch)
Stems = A (straight stitch)
Leaves = Q (ribbon stitch)

### Wisteria

Flowers = K (French knot, 1–2 wraps), U (French knot, 2–3 wraps)
Leaves = P (ribbon stitch)

### Delphiniums

Petals = N, O or R (straight stitch, ribbon stitch)
Leaves = V (ribbon stitch), C (straight stitch)

### Hydrangeas

Flowers = M (French knot, 1–2 wraps)
Leaves = V (ribbon stitch)

### Lavender

Flowers = T (straight stitch)
Stems = A (straight stitch)
Leaves = Q (ribbon stitch)

*Grass* = L (straight stitch, ribbon stitch), A (straight stitch)

# GHOST

## by Kari Mecca

### This design uses

*Bullion knot – detached chain combination,
Chain stitch, Couching, Detached chain,
Ribbon stitch, Straight stitch*

### Ribbon embroidery index

Bullion knot – detached chain
combination 8
Ribbon stitch 23

## Materials

### Threads & ribbon

*DMC stranded cotton*
A = 310 black
B = 317 pewter grey
*YLI silk ribbon 7mm (⁵⁄₁₆") wide*
C = 50cm (20") no. 3 white

### Needles

No. 8 straw (milliner's) needle
No. 18 chenille needle

## Order of work

Use the no. 18 chenille needle for the
ribbon work and the straw needle for
the thread embroidery.

### Ghost

Beginning at the neck and stitching
upwards, work a bullion knot – detached
chain combination stitch for the head.
Anchor the stitch at an angle. For the
body, work a longer stitch in the same
manner, stitching downwards.

Embroider a ribbon stitch for each
arm, bringing the ribbon to the front
each time just behind the upper body.

Stitch two detached chains for the
eyes. Work a straight stitch for the
mouth and couch it into a curve.

### Chain

Embroider the chain in chain stitch,
working across the arms and body.

### Embroidery key

*All thread embroidery is worked with
one strand.*

#### Ghost

Head and body = C (bullion knot –
detached chain combination, 1 wrap)
Arms = C (ribbon stitch)
Eyes = A (detached chain)
Mouth = A (straight stitch, couching)

*Chain* = B (chain stitch)

# FLOWER FAIRY

## by Kari Mecca

### This design uses

*Couching, Bullion knot – detached chain
combination, Detached chain, French knot,
Loop stitch, Ribbon stitch, Straight stitch*

### Ribbon embroidery index

Bullion knot – detached chain
combination 8
Detached chain 12
Loop stitch 19
Ribbon stitch 23
Straight stitch 33

## Materials

### Threads & ribbons

*DMC stranded cotton*
A = 224 vy lt shell pink
B = 317 pewter grey
*YLI silk ribbon 7mm (⁵⁄₁₆") wide*
C = 1m (39 ½") no. 5 blush pink
D = 1m (39 ½") no. 125 powder blue
E = 1m (39 ½") no. 156 cream
*YLI silk ribbon 4mm (³⁄₁₆") wide*
F = 50cm (20") no. 148 hazelnut brown
*YLI spark organdy ribbon 5mm (³⁄₁₆") wide*
G = 50cm (20") no. 01 pale pink

## Needles

No. 8 crewel needle
No. 18 chenille needle
No. 22 chenille needle

## Order of work

Use the no. 18 chenille needle for the 7mm (⁵⁄₁₆") ribbons and the no. 22 chenille needle for the 4mm and 5mm (³⁄₁₆") ribbons. The crewel needle is used for the thread embroidery.

### Fairy

Embroider the flower fairy following the step-by-step instructions on this page.

## Embroidery key

*All thread embroidery is worked with one strand.*

### Fairy

Wings = E (bullion knot – detached chain combination, 1 wrap, detached chain)
Wing highlights = G (straight stitch)
Head = C (detached chain)
Body = C (detached chain)
Arms and hands = C (straight stitch)
Legs = C (straight stitch)
Hair = F (straight stitch)
Eyes = B (French knot, 2 wraps)
Mouth = A (straight stitch, couching)

### Clothing

Top = D (straight stitch)
Skirt = D (ribbon stitch)
Shoes = D (straight stitch)
Hair bow = D (loop stitch, straight stitch)

1 **Wings.** Stitch a detached chain for the lower section and a bullion knot – detached chain combination stitch for the upper section.

2 For highlights, add two straight stitches to each upper wing and one to each lower wing.

3 **Body.** Beginning at the neck, work a detached chain for the head and then a slightly longer one for the body.

4 Work straight stitches for the arms and hands. Starting with the lower section, stitch two straight stitches for each leg.

5 **Hair.** Work ten straight stitches of varying lengths.

6 **Clothing.** Stitch two straight stitches for the top and two for the shoes.

7 Beginning at the waist each time, work five ribbon stitches for the skirt. Stitch a 13mm (½") loop stitch at the top of the head.

8 Flatten the loop and work a small straight stitch across the centre to form the hair bow.

9 **Face.** Add French knots for eyes. Work a straight stitch for the mouth. Couch in the middle, pulling it into a curve.
**Completed fairy.**

# SHEEP

## by Sarah Constantine

## This design uses
*French knot, Stem stitch, Straight stitch*

### Ribbon embroidery index
French knot 16
Straight stitch 33

## Materials

### Threads & ribbons

*Anchor stranded cotton*
A = 2 white
B = 240 vy lt Kelly green
*YLI silk ribbon 2mm (⅛") wide*
C = 80cm (31 ½") no. 94 lt Nile green
D = 30cm (12") no. 113 bright shell pink
E = 30cm (12") no. 121 dark
canary yellow
*YLI silk ribbon 4mm (³/₁₆") wide*
F = 30cm (12") no. 4 black
G = 40cm (16") no. 94 lt Nile green
*YLI silk ribbon 7mm (⁵/₁₆") wide*
H = 2m (2yd 7") no. 1 antique white
I = 20cm (8") no. 4 black

### Needles

No. 10 crewel needle
No. 18 chenille needle
No. 22 chenille needle

## Order of work

Use the no. 18 chenille needle for the
7mm (⁵/₁₆") ribbons and the no. 22
chenille needle for the other ribbons.
The crewel needle is used for all
thread embroidery.

### Sheep

Stitch the body beginning with an
outline of French knots placed close
together. Fill the body keeping the knots
as close together as possible. Embroider
the head with a single straight stitch,
keeping it flat to form the face. Work the
ears, legs and tail with straight stitches
using the narrow black ribbon. Create
each eye with two tiny straight stitches.

### Flowers

For each of the flowers, embroider five
straight stitches around a French knot
centre. The pink flowers have a yellow
centre and the yellow flowers have a
pink centre. Work the stems in
stem stitch.

### Foliage

Using the wider green ribbon, work the
leaves in angled straight stitches. Stitch
the grass using both widths of
green ribbon.

## Embroidery key

*All thread embroidery is worked with
one strand unless otherwise specified.*

### Sheep

Body = H (French knot, 1 wrap)
Face and ears = I (straight stitch)
Legs and tail = F (straight stitch)
Eyes = A (straight stitch)

### Flowers

Petals = D or E ( straight stitch)
Centre = D or E (French knot,
1 wrap)
Leaves = C (straight stitch)
Stems = B (2 strands, stem stitch)

### Foliage

Leaves = G (straight stitch)
Grass = C and G (straight stitch)

# INSECTS

## by Helen Dafter

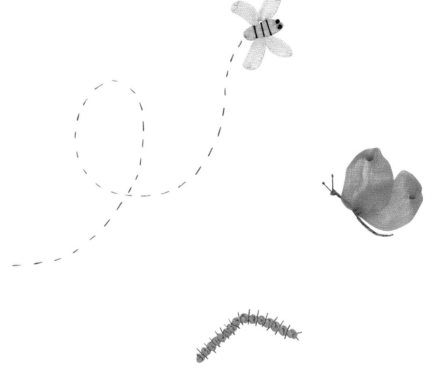

### This design uses

*French knot, Pistil stitch, Ribbon stitch,*
*Running stitch, Stem stitch, Straight stitch*

> **Ribbon embroidery index**
> French knot 16
> Ribbon stitch 23

## Materials

### Threads & ribbons

*Rajmahal Art silk*
A = 29 charcoal
B = 171 woodlands
C = 226 gothic grey
*YLI silk ribbon 4mm (³⁄₁₆") wide*
D = 20cm (8") no. 15 bright yellow
E = 50cm (20") no. 51 light antique gold
F = 20cm (8") no. 156 cream
*YLI spark organdy ribbon 13mm (½") wide*
G = 20cm (8") no. 21 sky blue

### Needles

No. 9 crewel needle
No. 18 chenille needle
No. 20 chenille needle

## Order of work

Use the no. 20 chenille needle when
working with the 4mm (³⁄₁₆") ribbons
and the no. 18 chenille needle when
working with the organdy ribbon. The
crewel needle is used for all
thread embroidery.

### Bee

Embroider a ribbon stitch for the body.
Bring the needle to the front at the tail
and take it to the back through the
ribbon at the head. Stitch the wings with
ribbon stitch, coming up beside the body
and down at the wing tips. Embroider
two French knots for the eyes and three
straight stitches for the body stripes.
Add the spiralling flight path with
running stitch.

### Butterfly

Work a line of stem stitch for the body
and then a French knot for the head.
Embroider two pistil stitches for
the antennae.

Stitch the wings in ribbon stitch,
working from the body to the wing tips.

### Caterpillar

For the body, work a closely packed row
of French knots. Work the legs and the
antennae in straight stitch.

## Embroidery key

*All thread embroidery is worked with
one strand unless otherwise specified.*

### Bee

Body = D (ribbon stitch)
Wings = F (ribbon stitch)
Eyes = A (French knot, 2 wraps)
Stripes = A (straight stitch)
Flight path = C (running stitch)

### Butterfly

Body = C (2 strands, stem stitch)
Head = C (2 strands, French knot,
2 wraps)
Antennae = C (pistil stitch)
Wings = G (ribbon stitch)

### Caterpillar

Body = E (French knot, 1 wrap)
Legs = B (straight stitch)
Antennae = B (straight stitch)

# SEAGULL

## by Kari Mecca

### This design uses

*Bullion knot – detached chain combination,*
*Detached chain, French knot, Ribbon stitch,*
*Straight stitch*

### Ribbon embroidery index

Bullion knot – detached chain
combination 8
Detached chain 12
Ribbon stitch 23
Straight stitch 33

## Materials

### Thread & ribbons

*DMC stranded cotton*
A = 310 black
*YLI silk ribbon 7mm (⁵⁄₁₆") wide*
B = 50cm (20") no. 3 white
*YLI silk ribbon 4mm (³⁄₁₆") wide*
C = 25cm (10") no. 147 gold

### Needles

No. 8 crewel needle
No. 18 chenille needle
No. 22 chenille needle

### Order of work

Use the no. 18 chenille needle for the
7mm (⁵⁄₁₆") ribbon and the no. 22
chenille needle for the 4mm (³⁄₁₆")
ribbon. The crewel needle is used for the
thread embroidery.

   Beginning at the neck, work a bullion
knot – detached chain combination
stitch for the body. Stitch a detached
chain for the head. Bring the ribbon to
the front through the body and work a
ribbon stitch for the wing.

   Embroider two tiny straight stitches,
which meet at the tip, for the beak. Work
a straight stitch for each leg and two
straight stitches for each foot.

   Add a black French knot for the eye.

### Embroidery key

*All thread embroidery is worked with
two strands.*

#### Seagull

Body = B (bullion knot – detached
chain combination, 1 wrap)
Head = B (detached chain)
Wing = B (ribbon stitch)
Beak = C (straight stitch)
Legs and feet = C (straight stitch)
Eye = A (French knot, 2 wraps)

---

# PENGUIN

## by Kari Mecca

### This design uses

*Bullion knot – detached chain combination,*
*Detached chain, French knot, Ribbon stitch,*
*Straight stitch*

### Ribbon embroidery index

Bullion knot – detached chain
combination 8
Detached chain 12
Ribbon stitch 23
Straight stitch 33

## Materials

### Thread & ribbons

*DMC stranded cotton*
A = 310 black
*YLI silk ribbon 7mm (⁵⁄₁₆") wide*
B = 30cm (12") no. 3 white
C = 50cm (20") no. 47 navy
*YLI silk ribbon 4mm (³⁄₁₆") wide*
D = 20cm (8") no. 174 bright orange

### Needles

No. 8 crewel needle
No. 18 chenille needle
No. 22 chenille needle

## Order of work

Use the no.18 chenille needle for the 7mm (⁵⁄₁₆") ribbons and the no. 22 chenille needle for the 4mm (³⁄₁₆") ribbon. The crewel needle is used for the thread embroidery.

### Penguin

Using the navy ribbon, work a bullion knot – detached chain combination stitch for the body. Begin the stitch at the feet and anchor it at the neck. Change to the white ribbon and work a detached chain over the tip of the previous stitch for the head. Work a straight stitch, which covers the lower half of the first stitch, for the underbody. Using the navy ribbon, embroider a straight stitch across the top of the head. Pull the ribbon firmly so the stitch becomes very thin.

Stitch two ribbon stitches for the feet and two for the wings. Bring the ribbon to the front through the upper edge of the underbelly for the upper wing and behind the underbelly for the lower wing.

Embroider the beak with two straight stitches that share the same hole in the fabric at the tip. Finish the head with a French knot for the eye.

### Embroidery key

*All thread embroidery is worked with two strands.*

*Penguin*

Body = C (bullion knot – detached chain combination, 1 wrap),
B (straight stitch)
Head = B (detached chain),
C (straight stitch)
Feet and wings = C (ribbon stitch)
Beak = D (straight stitch)
Eye = A (French knot, 2 wraps)

# SEAL

## by Kari Mecca

### This design uses

*Bullion knot – detached chain combination, Detached chain, French knot, Ribbon stitch, Straight stitch*

## Materials

### Threads & ribbon

DMC stranded cotton
A = 310 black
B = 3811 vy lt teal
YLI silk ribbon 7mm (⁵⁄₁₆") wide
C = 1m (39 ½") no. 58 lt grey

### Needles

No. 8 crewel needle
No. 18 chenille needle

## Order of work

Use the chenille needle for the ribbon embroidery and the crewel needle for the thread embroidery.

### Seal

Embroider a bullion knot – detached chain combination stitch for the body. Work a detached chain for the head.

Each flipper is a ribbon stitch. Bring the ribbon to the front through the body for the upper front flipper and behind the body for the lower front flipper. Work the hind flippers as a pair of ribbon stitches.

Add a French knot for the eye and two straight stitches for the whiskers. Embroider two or three straight stitches side by side for the nose.

### Water

Using the teal thread, stitch five scattered detached chain stitches for the splashes of water.

### Embroidery key

*All thread embroidery is worked with one strand unless otherwise specified.*

*Seal*

Body = C (bullion knot – detached chain combination, 1 wrap)
Head = C (detached chain)
Flippers = C (ribbon stitch)
Eye = A (French knot, 2 wraps)
Nose and whiskers = A (straight stitch)

*Water* = B (2 strands, detached chain)

# The Patterns

## The following patterns are coloured for clarity and drawn to scale.

The drawings are simplified and are to be transferred onto the fabric as placement guides only. So that the ribbon work will cover any transferred markings, we have represented the position for the stitches with a simple line, the ends of which indicate the entry and exit points for the ribbon. In most instances, shapes worked with thread embroidery are represented with outlines, as these can be completely covered with the stitching.

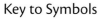

## Key to Symbols

| Knots and stitches | | Roses | Flowers and leaves |
|---|---|---|---|
| \ Ribbon stitch / Straight stitch | ⌐ Loop stitch | Cabbage rose | 🔵 Whipped straight stitch rose |
| ○ French knot or beading | ☐ Single loop stitch flower | (F) Folded ribbon rose | **Flowers and leaves** |
| ⊘ Colonial knot | Ψ Fly stitch | Gathered rose | Blossom bud |
| 〇 Bullion knot | Feather stitch | Spider web rose | Large blossom |
| Ϙ Detached chain | ϙ Pistil stitch | Stem stitch rose | Loop stitch flower |
| δ Twisted detached chain or ribbon rosebuds | ▣ Running stitch – colonial knot combination | Twirled ribbon rose | Loop straight stitch flower |
| | ᴥ Ribbon filler | | Pansy leaves |

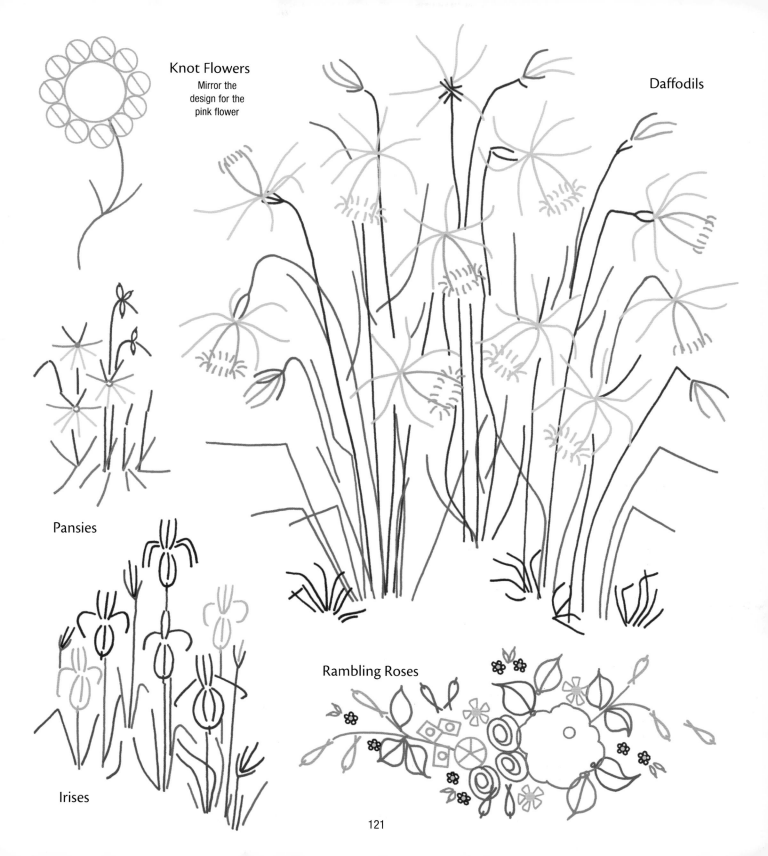

**Knot Flowers**
Mirror the
design for the
pink flower

Daffodils

Pansies

Irises

Rambling Roses

121

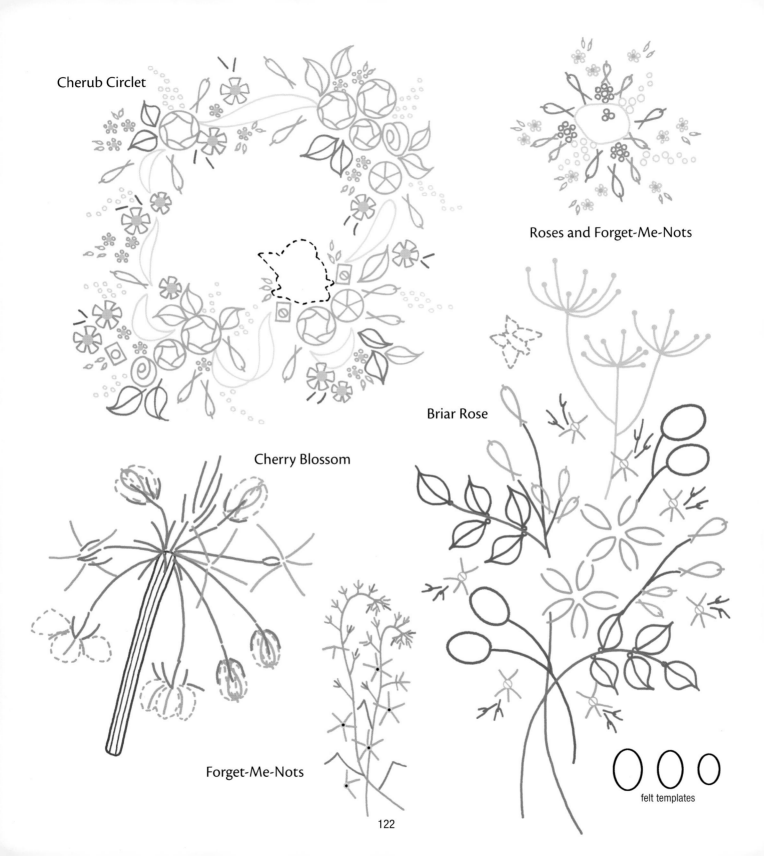

Cherub Circlet

Roses and Forget-Me-Nots

Briar Rose

Cherry Blossom

Forget-Me-Nots

felt templates

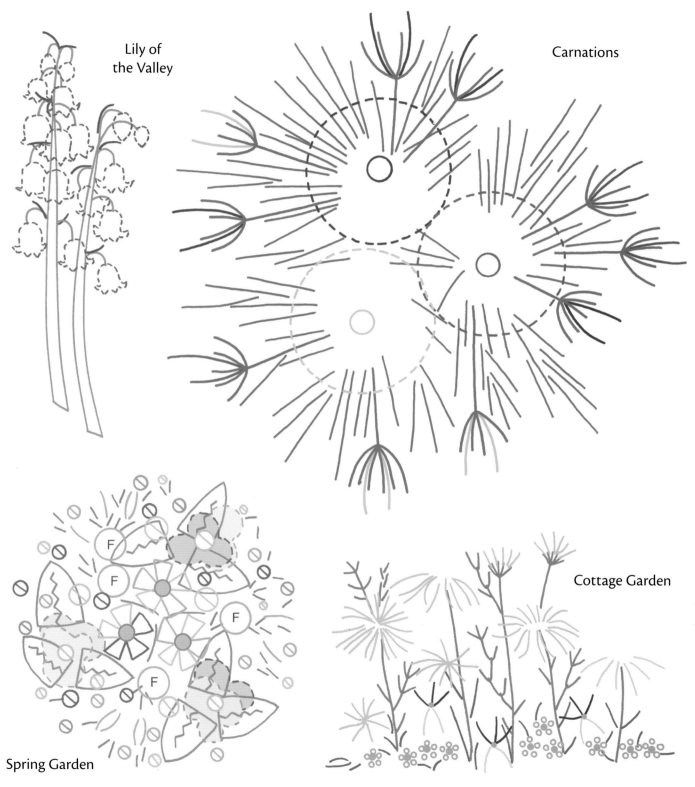

Lily of the Valley

Carnations

Cottage Garden

Spring Garden

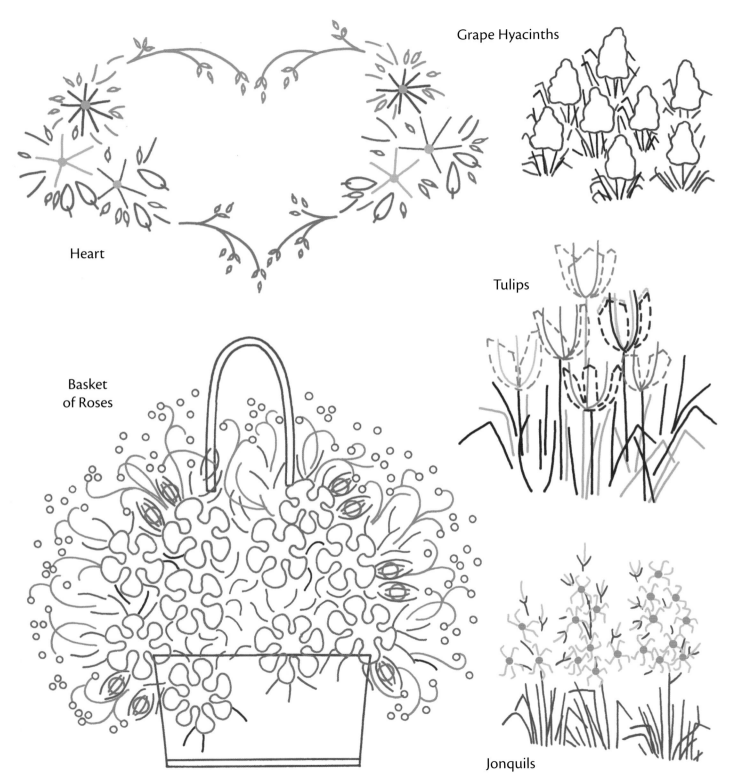

Grape Hyacinths

Heart

Tulips

Basket
of Roses

Jonquils

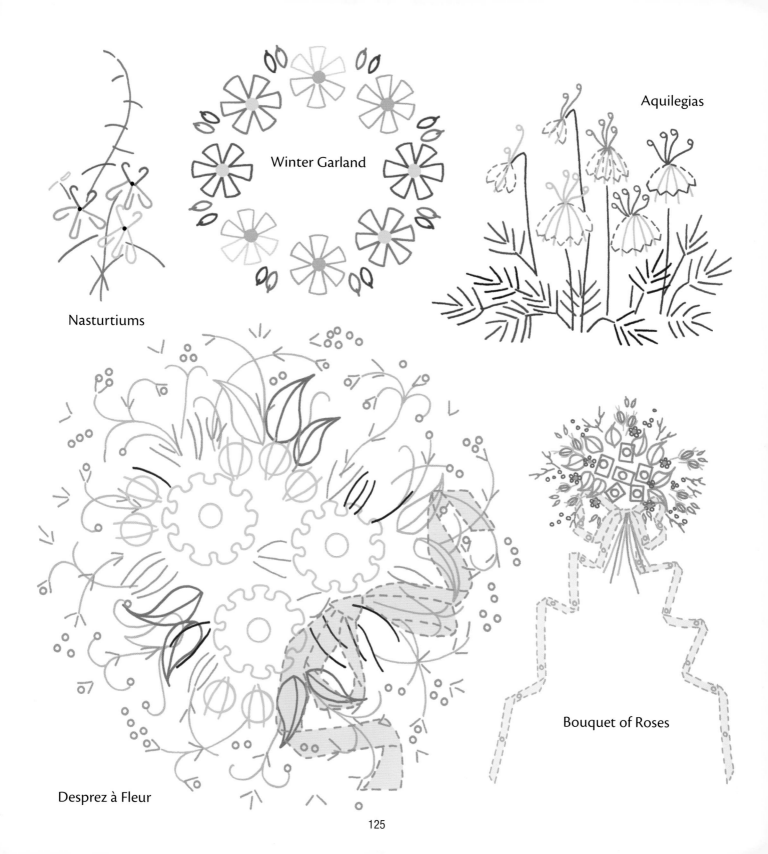

Nasturtiums

Winter Garland

Aquilegias

Desprez à Fleur

Bouquet of Roses

Victorian Bouquet

Small Daffodils

Snowdrops

126

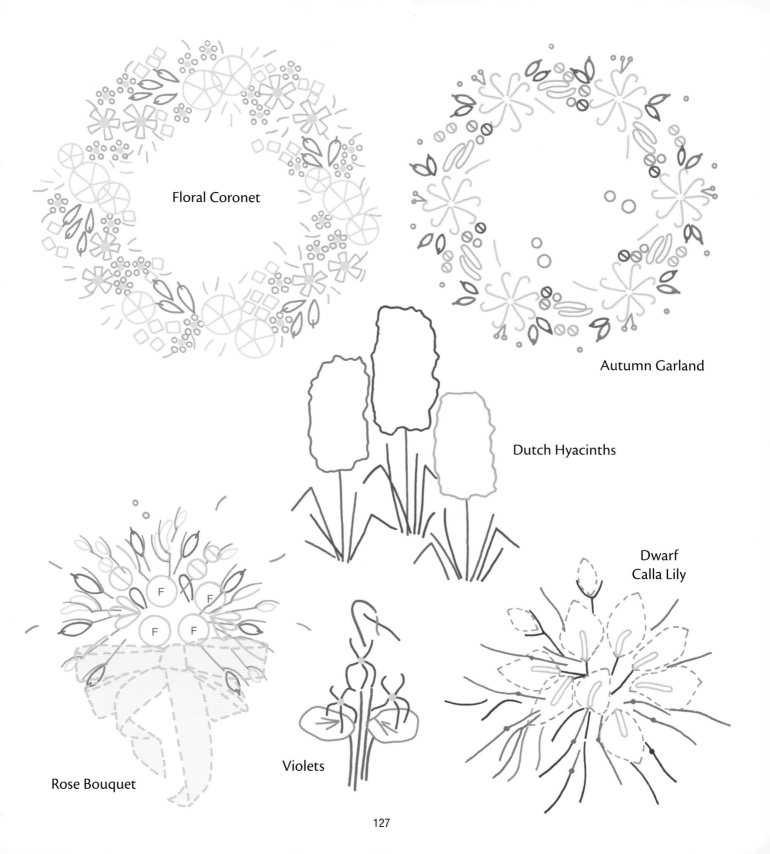

Floral Coronet

Autumn Garland

Dutch Hyacinths

Dwarf
Calla Lily

Rose Bouquet

Violets

127

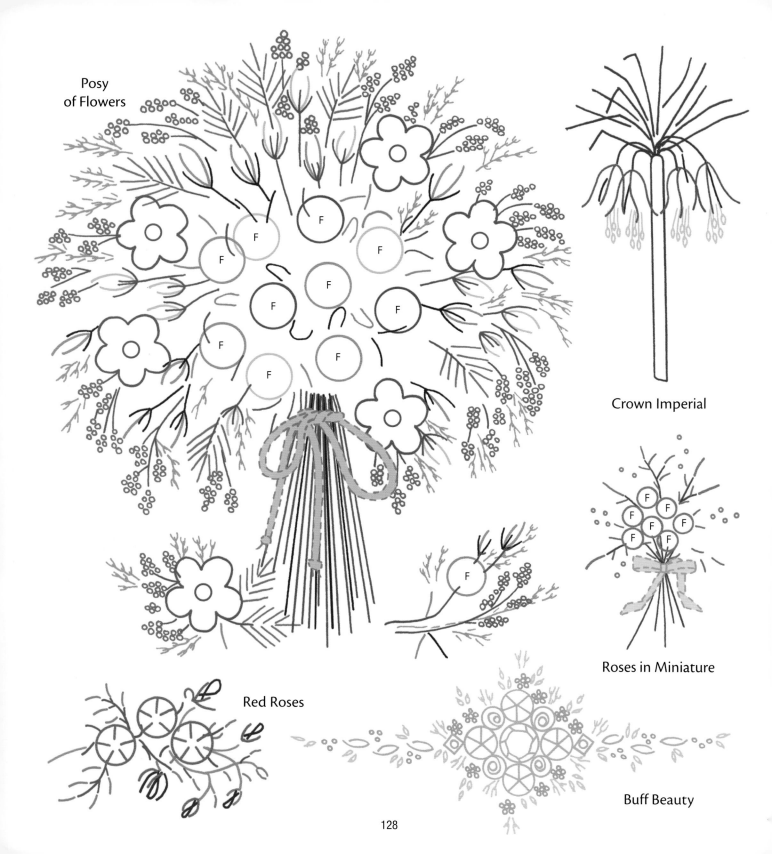

Posy of Flowers

Crown Imperial

Roses in Miniature

Red Roses

Buff Beauty

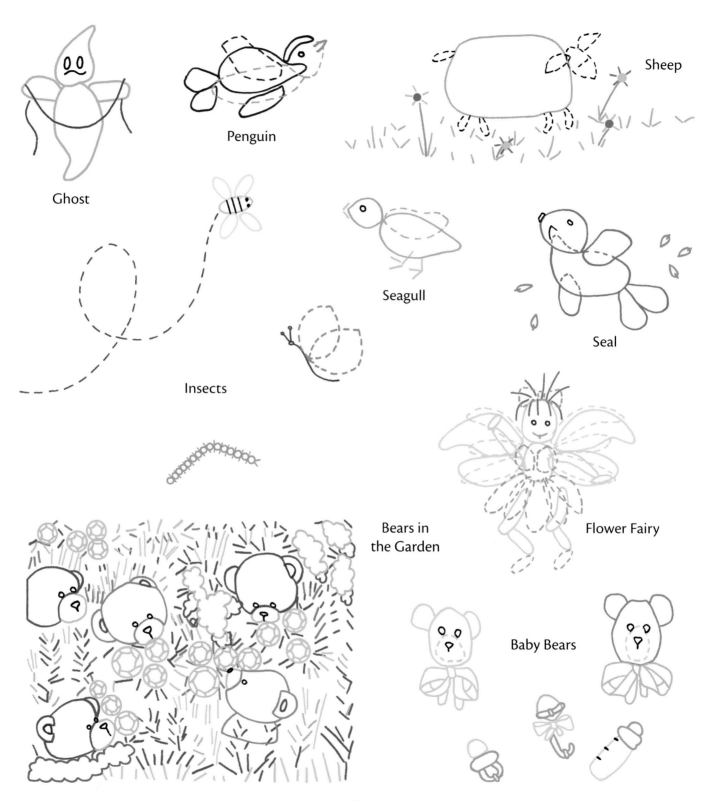

Ghost

Penguin

Sheep

Insects

Seagull

Seal

Bears in
the Garden

Flower Fairy

Baby Bears

# Index